FREDERIC REMINGTON: *Artist of the Old West*

FREDERIC REMINGTON

Artist of the Old West

WITH A BIBLIOGRAPHICAL CHECK LIST OF REMINGTON PICTURES AND BOOKS

BY

Harold McCracken

INTRODUCTION BY
JAMES CHILLMAN, JR.
DIRECTOR, MUSEUM OF FINE ARTS OF HOUSTON, TEXAS

J. B. LIPPINCOTT COMPANY

Philadelphia and New York

To

EMMA L. CATEN

who, more than anyone else,
has striven to keep alive
the memory of

FREDERIC REMINGTON

This book has been prepared in co-operation with
THE FREDERIC REMINGTON ESTATE
and
THE REMINGTON ART MEMORIAL

Introduction

ABOUT two years before the death of Frederic Remington, the critic Perriton Maxwell said this of him: "It is a matter of self-congratulation that in ringing down the final curtain on the great Wild West drama, the relentless course of empire has left us at least one auditor with skill and enthusiasm and courage enough to perpetuate on canvas and in enduring bronze the most inspiring phases of its colorful existence." Yet Remington was no native of the plains. He was born in New York state and as a boy the only indications of his future career were a love of the outdoors and a love for drawing. When, upon the death of his father, he set out for the West to seek fortune and adventure, his sketch book was always with him. In it he drew what he saw. The sketches, at first crude, then of greater technical skill, were always records of observed fact. By them we begin to understand why, in his limited field, he stands so far above his numerous imitators.

It is not difficult to understand the great popularity of Remington's works or to account for the praise lavishly given by many fellow artists and critics. His own words furnish the answer. "I paint for boys," he said, "boys from ten to seventy." The romantic adventure about which every boy dreams was made visible in accurately painted scenes done by a master storyteller. Almost without exception the high praise that is given Remington is directed at his power to tell a story, the authenticity of his depicted facts and his ability to draw accurately.

It is just as easy to understand his adverse critics who see in his storytelling and factual painting a definite limit to creative imagination and expression. Remington is dismissed as only an illustrator and his works as only illustrations. As such, to these critics, the works seem hardly worth the time necessary for examination. Frederic Remington was an illustrator, of that there is no doubt, but that his paintings are only illustrations is a more open question.

The thoughtful layman may well ask, "Just what is wrong with illustration?" or "Why is it considered less worthy than any other art forms?" If it is less worthy, then how can we account for the interest in Remington's work which has grown rather than diminished? Is it to be explained only by the glib statement that the great popularity of a work of art is almost a sure sign of its lack of high merit, or could it be that certain elements in Remington's works give them more lasting, more artistically important qualities which the layman senses but cannot explain?

The term "illustration" in itself should carry no derogatory meaning. After all Giotto and Masaccio were illustrators, as were Rembrandt and Hogarth. Illustration plays a necessary part in art expression, but it so happens that illustration by its very nature turns the attention of the spectator away from the work of art itself to the incident or thing which the work of art explains or records. The stronger the illustration the more is the interest of the spectator focused upon the subject or story. The painting or piece of sculpture becomes simply the means by which a fact or series of facts is explained. It places these facts in visible form so that they may be readily grasped and understood and by this very quality keeps the interest of the spectator upon the facts represented. No wonder it has been said that one picture is worth a thousand words.

However, it is quite evident to most people that a painting or a piece of sculpture by the arrangement of its forms or colors can express a thought, suggest a quality, even evoke a strong emotional response in the spectator irrespective of any subject or story that may be involved. In some cases the subject has so little relevance that it is abandoned completely. Forms and colors, like notes in music, can be used to suggest or to create a definite world without the need of depicting it literally.

But most of us, being what we are, respond most quickly to forms that we know or can recognize or at least can readily imagine. To us the strength of an artist does not lie in his ability to abandon the visible world, but in his ability to intensify its significance by selecting and choosing those forms which are most relevant to the thought or feeling to be expressed.

This sense of the relevant, of the significant, in general and in detail, was strongly developed in Frederic Remington and perhaps this sense, more than any other quality, makes his work an authoritative statement, one of the necessary factors of all great art.

Remington's formal art education was so brief that he might well be called a self-taught artist. It is true that he studied at the Yale Art School under J. Alden Weir. He did not like academic restrictions but he did like football. Professor Weir is said to have remarked that "Remington was a queer-looking art student as he frequently had his face and legs bandaged." Later after achieving some success with his pen-and-ink studies we find him going to the Art Students League in New York for additional training as if to correct certain technical deficiencies and develop his knowledge of other media. But by far the greater part of his technical development came from self-study and the personal observation of the methods of his contemporaries. His technical methods were never bound by the conventional art school practice of his day, but though they were unorthodox, nevertheless they were sound.

8

He was, or soon became, familiar with most art mediums: pen, crayon, watercolor and oil, but his desire to paint seriously did not appear until he was thirty. His interest in sculpture came even later in his life, but he brought to his modelling and casting an enthusiasm which quickly developed great technical skill.

His technical progress in each art medium he used followed the same general pattern, which was similar to the method by which he collected the material forming the background necessary to the creation of a work of art. This method was not new— it was the old one of collecting as many facts as possible about as many things as possible by means of innumerable notes, written and sketched. It seems to be used most in times when the intellectual curiosity of both artist and public is directed objectively at the natural world and usually produces a work of art in which the literary content or "story" is given importance.

Leonardo da Vinci followed this method so completely that his notes, perhaps, are more valuable than his more finished works. In some ways the same thing might be said of Remington. In his sketch notes we meet Remington the realist, Remington the analyst, the Remington whose keen observation could pick easily the most important out of a group of facts. His final work was seldom done on the spot but at a later time after all of the facts were noted and revaluated. Remington was not one to take his easel to the subject, rather he brought the subject to the easel. It is not surprising then to realize that most of his major paintings of the West were actually painted in his studio in the East.

That these pictures have the feeling of being painted on the spot is due to the fact that his notes and sketches were not done from hearsay evidence but were made by close contact with each subject and rich acquaintance with its background. It is true that Remington painted many events which he could not have seen and some which happened before he was born, such as his painting called the "Drawing of a Black Bean," now in the collection of the Museum of Fine Arts of Houston, and the water-color of "Custer's Last Stand" in the same museum. Remington was a boy of fifteen at the time of the massacre, but later he was with the United States Army of the West, and knew it well, as is amply attested in his illustrations for *Personal Recollections of General Miles*, and his *Frontier Sketches*.

Pen, crayon and water color lend themselves to note-taking. Remington's love for, and use of, the quick sketch in pencil or ink can be followed throughout his career. These sketches, some complete and some fragmentary, are the most interesting and revealing of his works and no understanding of his complete genius can be had without a careful consideration of them. But he was not content to depend upon his notes and sketches completely. His love of accuracy filled his studio with cowboy trappings. Indian costumes, ornaments, tools and weapons, objects of all sorts from many places served as source material for his work.

Largely because he had so many commissions as an illustrator, his first works in oil were usually in monochrome. To rich blacks, greys and whites were sometimes added tones of ochre or touches of brilliant reds, but always limited and restrained in amount. Many of these oils basically in black and white are among his strongest and most dramatic paintings. One of these, "The Infantry Square"* and also recorded as "The Battle" is not only an early oil but one of his most forceful works, strong and compact in composition, brilliant in technical execution.

It is evident that the use of monochrome was to facilitate reproduction in a day when color processes were both expensive and experimental, yet Remington finds in this relatively limited use of color one of his most powerful tools. In fact, when he does begin to use a full-color palette his oils give the feeling of a drawing carefully done, then lightly washed with color. His water colors are of the same nature. For all their charm and skillful execution they are essentially water-color drawings rather than water-color paintings.

Fundamentally, Remington is not a colorist; in fact he seems uninterested in color either as a resource in composition or to heighten emotional content. He uses it only as a help to factual representation. Perhaps it was this that made him aware of the Impressionists and their use of color to aid the solutions of the problems of light and luminosity. The "Pointillists," or broken-color Impressionists, seem to interest him most. These masters of light and air seem to suggest to him how the bright sunshine and luminous shadows of the Western spaces could be better painted. He experiments with their methods by breaking his purple shadows into touches of clear blue and red, he softens his precise draughtsmanlike outlines by brush strokes that cross rather than follow them, but never does he adopt this technique of Impressionism completely.

As his interest grows in the possibilities of the oil medium his brushwork becomes bolder and the pigments thicker and richer in application. The character of his color changes from that of the tinted black-and-white to that of a more complete color expression. However, color to enhance the telling of a story can be quite different from color as a basic element of design, and indicates to what qualities we must look to find Remington the artist.

His sculpture, as well, loses as much as it gains by the insistence on factual accuracy. It can be seen that in character the sculpture is really nothing but his painting given an actual rather than a suggested third dimension. It is pictorial rather than sculptural and its great virtue—the vivid suggestion of life and action—is often marred by persistent emphasis on literal detail. A coiled lariat of bronzed wire, a bridle with reins and thin metal ribbons, a "ten-gallon" hat waving in the air, tend to destroy rather than to build a unified effect. Yet in spite of aesthetic faults there is no technical fumbling; the medium of bronze is used with understanding and competence. It is

* *Harper's Monthly*, Sept., 1893.

easy to understand why he seldom if ever worked in wood or stone. The designs he created were possible only in cast metal. As a sculptor he seemed to think in bronze, or rather he thought first of his subject and then of the medium in which to fashion it. Bronze was the only answer.

This is quite a different viewpoint from that which creates an appropriate subject for metal and still different from the one which allows the material itself to dictate the subject or at least the manner in which the subject is treated. With Remington it was always the subject, the story, first.

This is just as true of his painting. His great interest in that world which he saw and experienced led him to create an adequate means to express it. His own words tell us how his need of expression developed his art vocabulary. "Without knowing exactly how to do it," he says, "I began to try to record some facts around me and the more I looked the more the panorama unfolded."

These words give us the clue to his rapid technical development. His technique was always sufficient to the needs of the story, but it was the story that mattered. Living through an age which saw the development of subjective painting, he remained impersonally objective. His rôle was that of the reporter, not the commentator. He seemed unconcerned with the significance of the incident which he portrayed or with its meaning as a symptom of a general condition in the march of events. This is well illustrated by one of his most popular and best-known paintings, "The Fight for the Waterhole" (Plate 12). Remington is an interested spectator of the episode, of how the persons concerned would appear under the particular conditions. He is neither for nor against the defenders. The effect on history, if this and other waterholes are won or lost, does not trouble him. He recounts the story and the reader may draw his own conclusions. He is a historian only in so far as he records events; the evaluation of their importance is left to others.

If morals are to be drawn from Remington's records the reader must draw them from the facts spread before his eyes. Rarely in his paintings does he seem to protest against evils or injustices, imagined or real, though he would have had opportunity, generously supplied, to collect material for such protests both from his life in the West and in Cuba during the Spanish American War. He does not dwell often on pain or tragedy. One of the few exceptions in his major works is the painting usually called "The Transgressor."† This deals with the horrible end of a small Mexican who, it seems, offended the Apaches, for which he was hung head downward over a cliff, suspended by one foot only. Even here the tale is told impersonally.

Remington espouses no cause, indulges in no social comments, nor is he interested in his personal reactions to the events he records. The manner in which he might be affected by his experiences is never shown in the character of his painting. Remington

† "Tio Juan Hanging There Dead," *Harper's Monthly*, Feb., 1893.

the man and Remington the artist can be seen more clearly by reading between the lines than by the lines themselves.

One of the most common approaches to art, certainly among occidental peoples, is the interest in factual knowledge; and to painting the interest in factual representation. Apelles received the plaudits of Athens when horses whinnied with delight on seeing his paintings of them, and Remington is acclaimed for his accurate recording of the things he sees. It was not the finished technique of his early pen sketches which started him on his way, for the brevity of his art training was all too apparent, but what got him his early commissions was the interest of the public in any fact that seemed authentic about the American Indian and the great West.

This interest in factual knowledge and representation was Remington's own approach, not only to the mastery of his technical means, but to the attainment of his artistic ends—the pictorial record, the pictorial reconstruction of a vanishing world. So intent was he on this vanishing world and so intent have been his adherents upon this past epoch in American history that the brilliance of his art is all but lost in the brilliance of his storytelling.

Some people tell stories so well that their method of telling becomes identified with themselves, and finally they are identified with their stories. This was Remington; his personality becomes absorbed by the personality of the story. We accept the content of his picture as fact, so he insists that, in so far as possible, this accepted fact be correct. For this alone his paintings become invaluable documents. This accuracy of detail is one of the reasons for the great popularity of his works, a popularity so great that it has caused many forgeries. Strangely enough the detection of these forgeries is often made by means of the factual accuracy of the originals.

If there is one weakness in Remington's storytelling it is not his love for accurate fact but his incurable romanticism. The romance of the Pioneer West, the romance of war, the romance and thrill of adventure, all are told, but the heartbreak, the suffering, the sting of defeat seldom appear. In his painting "The Emigrants" (Plate 15) can be seen one of the tragic incidents in the conquering of the West, but with all the accuracy of fact, precision of detail and the simulated action, the spectator is sure that the hard-riding Indian is never going to stab the young pioneer, or if he does the youth will recover and the West will be won. Here perhaps is another reason for the popularity of Remington's work. Most Americans, too, are incurable romantics, at least in what they like in art.

In his paintings Remington is a romantic storyteller, in his sketches a realist in search of facts. Add these together and one sees why he has been acclaimed the great chronicler of a vanished epoch. Yet Remington is more than the teller of well-told tales; he is more than the careful collector of interesting and valuable data.

Thousands of years ago the cave men of Western Europe began to make records

12

of the things they saw which were of vital importance to their lives. They did this by modelling, then drawing, then engraving the images of the animals which they hunted for food and clothing. Finally they painted, ceremoniously, the images of these animals on the walls of the dim interiors of their caves. By this time they had left the factual record far behind and reached the point of a great pictorial convention. As the earlier works amaze us by their precise recording of facts, so the later paintings astound us by the great economy of means by which effects are obtained and ideas communicated. The particular fact has been transformed into a universal truth. A bison is painted charging down the wall. It no longer is a certain bison; it becomes a pictorial symbol for all bison. The subject has been so well understood that its form, its action, its very nature is made visible by the most rigid economy of lines and color masses and a selection of only the facts essential to complete comprehension.

If Remington's work is closely examined, an almost parallel progression can be seen in his relatively short lifetime as an artist. First literal and exacting in his search for fact, Remington like the ancient engraver showed the legs of a running animal in positions that the average eye does not observe but which are verified by the slow-motion picture. He gradually developed the surety of touch and the economy of means which leads to a clear, concise and direct pictorial statement. Perhaps this is what Remington meant when he asked to be remembered as one who "knew the horse." Of all of his records, of all of his stories, the story of the horse is told the best.

If it is possible to point to the quality that makes Remington stand ahead of his followers and imitators or to that which causes him to be called "the foremost American painter in his chosen field," it will not be Remington the illustrator to whom we will look, nor to Remington the pictorial historian, but to Remington the artist. The difference lies not in technique, for able as he was he was no more talented than many others, but in his power of selection and his sense of the significant. He was able to select and to use only those forms which would emphasize the fundamental meaning of the story—seen romantically or not—and aid in its simple, honest and direct telling.

Perhaps this is why Frederic Remington and his art have become to the people of the United States symbols of that vanished world of romance and adventure which ever lives in their hearts.

JAMES CHILLMAN, JR.

Foreword

IT IS A CURIOUS fact that Frederic Remington, whose work has been so well known to three generations and loved by literally all sorts of people, has never been honored by a definitive biography. The following pages tell the most complete story of his life yet to be published. The book is the result of a number of years of pleasant effort in assembling, correlating and corroborating the material on which it is based. The writer has drawn on Remington's own books, articles, diaries, etc., and the sketchy bits of information about him which have appeared in the writings and letters of his contemporaries. But it is one of the happy inevitabilities of such work that it benefits most from the generous help of people who themselves knew the subject intimately. To these the writer wishes to make grateful acknowledgment.

A large part of the intimate biographical story has been provided by Miss Emma L. Caten, younger sister of Mrs. Frederic Remington. From the day she cried at their wedding, until the day of Frederic Remington's sudden and untimely death, Miss Caten spent a great deal of her time in their home, and was the couple's closest friend and confidante. Since the death of the artist and his wife, she has devoted a large part of her life to help foster and perpetuate the memory of her distinguished brother-in-law. As executrix and administratrix of the Remington Estate, Miss Caten has been responsible for the preservation of Frederic Remington's personal papers, diaries, notebooks, copyrights and a considerable amount of his work, which she has deposited in the Remington Art Memorial at Ogdensburg, New York. All this material has been made available to the writer. As Frederic Remington had but few intimate friends, most of whom are now gone, and intently avoided being interviewed even at the height of his career, comparatively little about him has ever appeared in print, and this has contained a good many inaccuracies and misrepresentations. He was not much of a letter writer and even the letters he wrote were mostly undated. In view of these difficulties, it is doubtful if such a book as this could have been possible if it had not been for the assistance of Emma L. Caten.

Another who contributed much original material, and substantiated or discredited other information, is the late John C. Howard, of Ogdensburg. He not only knew

Frederic Remington as a boy, but throughout the artist's life he continued to enjoy his closest friendship and confidence. He accompanied Remington on a number of his trips to the West and deep into the back country of Old Mexico; they were companions during the summers that Remington spent on the St. Lawrence. Howard probably spent more time with him, and knew him more intimately, than did any other man. It was John Howard's interest and financial assistance which were largely responsible for the establishment of the Remington Art Memorial. Several years before his death, Mr. Howard supplied this writer with some of the facts which have gone into the book, which otherwise would have been lost for the record.

Others—some no longer living—who have in one way or another contributed to this story of Frederic Remington and his work are: Poultney Bigelow, his classmate at Yale, purchaser (as editor of *Outing Magazine*) of some of his earliest work, and his companion on trips to North Africa, Europe and in the Spanish American War; Owen Wister, Theodore Roosevelt, Julian Ralph, Augustus Thomas, Riccardo Bertelli, F. Wellington Ruckstull, Franklin R. Little, Albert P. Newell, Miss Ursula Hornbrook, Charles P. Rogers, Walter G. Kellog, Lawrence F. Cuthbert, Charles P. Lyon, E. Walter Latendorf, H. Conrad McCracken and a number of others whose names are referred to during the course of the following pages.

Acknowledgment also is made to Harper & Brothers, P. F. Collier & Son, Appleton-Century & Company, Charles Scribner's Sons and Houghton, Mifflin & Company for their kind co-operation and permission to use certain material reproduced in this book.

HAROLD McCRACKEN

Contents

CONTENTS

Illustrations

LINE DRAWINGS

HALFTONE REPRODUCTIONS

PHOTOGRAPHS FROM BRONZES

FREDERIC REMINGTON: *Artist of the Old West*

CHAPTER I

Chronicler of the West

FREDERIC REMINGTON was considerably more than a painter and sculptor. Whatever academic excellence may be attributed to what he accomplished in paint, ink, clay and bronze, is transcended by its value as a documentary record and contribution to the early history of our great West. His work constitutes one of the most complete pictorializations of that most spectacular phase of the American scene—from the days when white men began to carve an empire out of a wilderness, to the days when the once noble red man had become but an ugly caricature of his conquerors. To record that wild and colorful epoch for permanent preservation was the thesis of Frederic Remington's career.

All the vital vestiges of that era have disappeared. The vast plains and prairies have been plowed under. The great expanses of primeval forests have in large part been cut down or burned. Lakes have been drained and disfigured. Swift rivers have been deprived of their picturesqueness and put into harness to create power more mysterious than the most imaginative Indian medicine man ever dared to dream about. Even mountain shapes have been distorted in the feverish search for minerals and for faster ways to get from one place to another. The great herds of wild animals are gone. Probably a hundred million or more buffalo, which have become something of a symbol of North America, were slaughtered for food, hides and mere sport. The vast numbers of antelope, moose, elk and most of the other wild animals are gone. The black bear has become a beggar of candy and tidbits, and even "Old Ephraim" the grizzly bear, once the terrible *horribilis*, has lost nearly all the ferocious truculence of his former days and runs away with the heart of a coyote.

The Indian has lost all of his once primitive majesty and stealthy terror. Even among his own people, such things as the scalp dance and the warpath are as much forgotten as last summer's sunshine. Gone also are the village circles of buffalo-skin tepees that once added a touch of colorful decoration to the bank of many a wilderness river. The slow cavalcade of covered wagons has been replaced by the streamlined train and passenger plane. The unshaven, buckskin-clad frontiersman, trapper, trader, trooper and pioneer homeseeker, who feared nothing that stalked the good earth in the form of redskin, beast or devil, has been replaced by the traveling salesman, college professor, butter-and-egg man and labor leader.

Not all that is gone was good, nor is all bad because it is new—but the Old West is gone beyond recall, and nostalgia for things past seems always to increase in direct ratio to the rush of progress into a new and different future. Remington to a rare and satisfying degree captured that Old West, preserving for all time its vivid colorfulness and the vitality of the men, the animals and the scenes that made up its picturesque parade. It is therefore only natural, as the years go by, that we should find an increasing interest in his work as well as in the man himself.

Frederic Remington and his work are by no means a new discovery, nor have we just come to realize the contribution which he has made to the interpretive history of the American scene. He may have been unduly neglected during the past generation or so, but he was not without prophets even in his own day.

As President of the United States, Theodore Roosevelt, paid the following tribute to Remington in a letter of July 17, 1907, sent to the editor of *Pearson's:*

> He is, of course, one of the most typical artists we have ever had, and he has portrayed a most characteristic and yet vanishing type of American life. The soldier, the cowboy and rancher, the Indian, the horses and the cattle of the plains, will live in his pictures and bronzes, I verily believe, for all time.

There were a good many other contemporary notables who had words of high praise for Remington's work. Among these, and by no means the least, was Owen Wister: "No artist until Remington has undertaken to draw so clearly the history of a people," he wrote in *Collier's,* March 18, 1905:

> This is surely enough; but he stands for certain other things, both great and definite. He has pictured the red man as no one else has pictured him. He has told his tragedy completely. He has made us see at every stage this race which our conquering race has dispossessed, beginning with its primeval grandeur, and ending with its squalid degeneration under the influence of our civilized manners.
>
> Next, while recording the red man in his way, Remington has recorded the white man who encountered him—recorded this man also in every stage from dignity to sordid squalor. Pioneers, trappers, cowboys, miners, prospectors, gamblers, bandits—the whole motley rout goes ineffaceably into Remington's pages.
>
> And, finally, he has not forgotten Nature herself. The mystery of the untouched plains and the awe of the unscaled mountains have been set down by him not only truthfully, but with potent feeling and imagination.

Remington is not merely an artist, he is a national treasure. And if it ever should occur to the not always discerning minds of academic institutions that Remington should be crowned at their hands, I should like to hear him receive his degree in these words: "Frederic Remington, Draughtsman, Historian, Poet."

There were others before him who drew and painted cowboys, Indians, horses and the Western scene, and there have been a good many who have done so since, but there is no other name which symbolizes our wild Old West as does Frederic Remington's.

"We almost forget," wrote Julian Ralph in *Harper's Weekly* of July 20, 1895,

that we did not always know the little army of rough riders of the plains, the sturdy lumbermen of the forests, the half-breed canoeman, the dare-devil scouts, the be-fringed and be-feathered red man, and all the rest of Remingtoniana that must be collected some day to feast the eye, as Parkman and Roosevelt and Wister satisfy the mind.

As will be seen through the following pages, success came no more easily to Remington than it does to most young artists, in spite of the appreciation of many notable contemporaries. There were years when failure and struggle were the rule and the academic nabobs were grudging in their recognition—and he died suddenly at the height of his career and when his work was taking on new and perhaps richer dimensions.

CHAPTER II

Beginning of the Trail

FREDERIC SACKRIDER REMINGTON was born in Canton, New York, on the first day of October, 1861; the son of Seth Pierrepont Remington and Clara Bascomb Sackrider Remington.

Seth and Clara had been married in January of the same year Frederic was born and the marriage joined two of the district's leading families. Perhaps because in those days several generations more willingly lived under the same roof than they do today, the young couple were living with Seth's father, the Reverend Samuel W. Remington, Universalist clergyman in Canton, at the birth of their first and only child.

In 1856 Seth Remington and William B. Goodrich had established the *St. Lawrence Plaindealer*, a newspaper which has continued to serve Canton and the surrounding countryside for almost a century. Seth was a fiery and excitable young man, with strong views, political and otherwise, all of which characteristics were, at that time particularly, almost indispensable to a successful newspaperman. The paper prospered, but Seth's patriotism was stronger than his wordly ambition, and when the Civil War began he neglected his paper to recruit a company for the regiment known as Swain's Cavalry, named after its commander, John R. Swain, which later became the famous fighting Eleventh New York Cavalry. When Frederic was but two months old Seth Remington sacrificed his business interests and his newly created family life and went to war with the regiment he had helped to establish.

After a few months Clara Remington took her young son to make their home with her own parents, the Henry L. Sackriders, who also lived in Canton. Here, with his maternal grandparents, Frederic Remington spent the earliest years of his life.

Seth Pierrepont Remington spent four long years as a cavalryman in the Civil War. He saw much fighting in the western campaigns in Tennessee and Mississippi, and returned to Canton a lieutenant colonel, with a distinguished military record. He re-

HARPER'S WEEKLY.
A
JOURNAL OF CIVILIZATION.

Vol. XXX.—No. 1555.
Copyright, 1886, by Harper & Brothers.

NEW YORK, SATURDAY, OCTOBER 9, 1886.

TEN CENTS A COPY.
$4.00 PER YEAR, IN ADVANCE.

IN FROM THE NIGHT HERD
An early example of the type of picture for which Remington later became best known

purchased the *St. Lawrence Plaindealer* and again settled down to the peaceful life of a family man. On his return from war, Seth found his four-year-old son big for his age, strong and active, with Seth's own impetuosity, high spirits, creative urge and love of adventure. Frederic inherited his sturdy physique from his mother's family.

The boy was very early at home everywhere in the wooded hills and valleys around Canton. When it came to fishing, hunting, climbing trees, hiking, swimming, boxing or just playing, red-faced, sandy-haired Frederic invariably excelled companions much older than himself. This leadership among his fellows, however, did not extend inside the school doors. He had no use at all for the confinement of a classroom and frequently the rod was used by his father as well as his teachers in an effort to convince him that the three R's were a necessity in every boy's life.

But the stories of Indians and high adventure in the glamorous land beyond the Mississippi which were told at the dinner table or in the parlor of nearly every Eastern home, found him an ardent student. That these stories made a deep impression upon Fred Remington is a part of the family tradition. For instance, there is the account of the time he sat astride a screaming playmate, much his senior in age, and cut the hair entirely off the victim's head while enacting a too realistic game of Indian scalping.

Frederic's skill and daring as a swimmer were the envy of all his playmates. The near-by Little River, especially where it flows into the Grasse River, was a favorite swimming place for the boys of Canton; and even as a small boy of seven or eight, Frederic was always among the first to brave the icy water in the early spring and the last to leave it in the chill of fall. His enthusiasm was not shared by his mother who unavailingly remonstrated, usually after the damage had been done. "If mother had only felt my hair she would have known it hadn't got that way carrying my books home from school," he would say years later. "But sometimes I wonder now if she didn't really know."

Two other interests were straws in the wind of the future. Horses held for him an unrivalled fascination; and he never ceased attempting to draw. Perhaps admiration for his cavalry-colonel father was at the bottom of his love for horses, and it is certain that his father encouraged his boyhood artistic efforts. His mother, a practical woman, had other, definite ideas; her son was to become a successful man well endowed with this world's goods, and she was never to be persuaded, even after his first modest triumphs, that success as an artist could compare with success as a businessman.

When he was not swimming, fishing or otherwise occupied in the out-of-doors, much of his time was spent around the local fire department, helping to care for the horses that raced the fire-fighting apparatus to Canton's occasional conflagrations. He was officially made "Mascot of Engine House No. 1" at the age of ten, with a fireman's hat all his own, and posed with the company for the local photographer.

The margins of his schoolbooks were sadly defaced by quantities of crude drawings in spite of no lack of proper sketch books in which to put down as best he could the things he saw or dreamed about. Horses, soldiers, wild Indians, things near and remote—the child struggled to delineate them all. Several of his sketch books—one of them, intended for an elegant autograph album, but firmly marked on the cover FINE ART—NOT AUTOGRAPHS, by the youthful artist—are preserved in the Remington Art Memorial at Ogdensburg and others are owned by private collectors.

Early in the seventies, when Frederic was eleven, Colonel Remington was appointed Collector of the Port of Ogdensburg on the St. Lawrence River, and the family moved from Canton. The two towns were within easy distance, and through frequent visits to his grandparents the boy kept in close touch with his old friends and the familiar stamping ground of his early adventures.

He attended the public schools of Ogdensburg and the Vermont Episcopal Institute in Burlington, Vermont; and in the fall of 1876 he was sent to the Highland Military Academy in Worcester, Massachusetts. His father, out of his experience as a soldier, looked upon military training as most valuable in the proper formation of character. Probably there were other valid reasons why the strict discipline of such schooling was considered a suitable prescription for this high-spirited youngster.

In spite of the intense interest he later developed in military men and the life they followed, at thirteen Frederic openly rebelled against the rigid regulations of the military academy. Restrictions of any kind were hateful to him, and he expressed his revolt actively by running away. The severe punishment which followed this escapade did nothing to lessen his dislike of military discipline, though he apparently resigned himself to the fact that the powers-that-be were too strong for him. Before the end of his course he had won the friendship of his fellow-cadets and even of his instructors. He was described as a "lazy" student, yet he did well in his schoolwork, especially in English, and thoroughly enjoyed military drill and athletics while doing his utmost to circumvent the discipline that went with them.

The principal interests of his life remained unchanged and the sketch books filled while he was at Worcester were largely devoted to mounted Indians in battle with American troopers. He found a kindred spirit in Scott Turner of Augusta, Maine, whose letters to one of Remington's classmates were liberally embellished by sketches. Scott and Frederic never met, but a lively correspondence began with a letter from Frederic:

Highland Military Academy, March 3, 1877

FRIEND SCOTT—Having seen some of your drawings which you sent Wilder, I am desirous of opening a correspondence with you. I hope you will honor me with your sanction. I am the fortunate possessor of one of your drawings, entitled "Where is the Cap't?" You draw splendidly, and I admire your mode of shading, which I cannot get the "hang" of. Your favorite subject is soldiers. So is mine; but, mind you, I do not pretend to compare my drawings with yours. I can draw almost as good as Wilder. If you will please to send me a sheet of pictures such as you sent Wilder, I will do my best to draw a little cadet life at the Highland Military Academy.

Yours truly,

F. S. REMINGTON.*

In another letter sent to Scott Turner, he tells about himself:

I don't amount to anything in particular. I can spoil an immense amount of good grub at any time in the day. I am almost as bad as Wilder, who is acknowledged to be the "baddest" man in school in that line. I go a good man on muscle. My hair is short and stiff, and I am about five feet eight inches and weigh one hundred and eighty pounds. There is nothing poetical about me. . . .

Wilder and myself have been under arrest for the last few days. We marched into the armory—I with the saber that David killed Goliath with and Wilder with an old rusty musket. I don't swear much, although it is my weak point, and I have to look my letters over carefully to see if there is any cussing in them. I never smoke—only when I can get treated—and I never condescend to the friendly offer of "Take something old hoss?"

Apparently Scott was not so single-minded as Frederic, for later he received the protest, "Don't send me any more women or any more dudes. Send me Indians, cowboys, villains, or toughs. These are what I want."

It was during one of the vacations from the military academy that Frederic made his first serious attempt at painting. His imagination having been fired by the accounts of Roman warfare with the barbarians, he placed in the forefront of his canvas a Gallic chieftain bound by chains to a pillar in a bleak Roman cavern, guarded by a Roman soldier in the background. The barbaric captive displays unsubdued fierceness, and the chains that bind him seem puny in comparison to the primitive brawn of his broad hairy chest, muscular arms and legs. In spite of its crudities, the painting is vigorous and animated, a not unworthy precursor of the future.

Frederic improvised a studio in his uncle's barn in Canton, because it provided a suitable place to pose his favorite models, and many a neighbor's carriage horse was borrowed or temporarily appropriated for the young artist's purposes. The discovery of paint was an exciting one and he flung himself into the study of it with the same wholehearted enthusiasm and determination to succeed that he brought to everything which caught his interest.

* Orin Edson Crooker, "A Page from the Boyhood of Frederic Remington," Collier's, Sept. 17, 1910.

CHAPTER III

A Young Man Goes West

WHEN he was just approaching his seventeenth birthday, in the fall of 1878, Frederic was sent to Yale. There is no documentary evidence that he startled any of the Yale professors with his scholarly enthusiasm or an aptitude for becoming a tycoon of American finance or industry, as his mother so desired. But the less than two years that he remained at Yale were not entirely wasted. He enrolled as an art student and won considerable fame as a football player.

The Yale Art School had but recently been established and the class consisted of only two students. The other was Poultney Bigelow, who was to become well known as a writer and editor, and friend of Kaiser Wilhelm II. The studio classroom was a dingy basement, with the artistic atmosphere supplied by a none too impressive assortment of plaster casts of antique sculpture. The first art lesson was based on the Faun of Praxiteles. It was hardly a sympathetic or inspiring atmosphere for young Remington's particular talents and the gloomy hours he spent there may have had a good deal to do with his settled distaste for academic art courses with their burdensome emphasis on European masters and techniques.

Poultney Bigelow conceived the idea of converting the Yale *Courant* into an illustrated college weekly, the first in America, with his classmate contributing some of the art work. One of a series of cartoons captioned "College Riff-Raff," which appeared on November 2, 1879, over the initials "FR," was the first published Remington. Possibly a self-portrait, it showed a student football player much battered and bandaged sitting in a dormitory room with a liniment bottle on the table beside him. Crude though it was, Bigelow insisted that it was "truly Yalensian—and therefore encouraged new subscribers and fresh advertisements for the *Yale Courant.*"

Fred Remington was better known at Yale as a football player than as either a student or an artist. He made the Varsity team which became celebrated because it was captained by a rather slender, moustachioed young classmate of Remington's, who later became football's foremost authority and exponent—Walter Camp. Remington won the special notice of the sports writers as an outstanding forward in the traditional Thanksgiving game against Princeton. However disillusioned he may have been by the formal study of art as practiced at Yale, the long football season was something he could look forward to with eagerness. Football was a rough and comparatively haphazard game in the seventies, in which a boy of Remington's temperament could find release.

He had spent less than two years at Yale when, in 1880, his father died, leaving him a modest inheritance sufficient to provide at least a temporary feeling of independence. To his mother's great disappointment he decided not to return to college the next year. Thanks to his father's political activity on behalf of the Republican Party, Fred procured a clerical position on the staff of the Governor of New York State, but was soon bored. In spite of his mother's alarmed protests that it was high time he settled down, he quit this job and started groping around in a restless attempt to find a way to follow the intangible distant urge which seemed always to be calling to him.

From his experience at Yale he had gained little more than a knowledge of two artists whose work he admired—Jean Baptiste Edouard Detaille and Alphonse Marie de Neuville, both of whom were noted for the meticulous accuracy with which they pictured military life, especially scenes from the recent Franco-Prussian War. The realism and exactitude of Detaille's and De Neuville's drawing of horses and men in action were a mark to shoot at, but hard for a beginner to hit. His impatience and restlessness increased and he became uncertain of his ambitions and his talent alike. He took jobs and gave them up, unable to endure the monotony and confinement of office work, and equally unable to stay away from pencil and brush for long at a time.

Then, in the summer of 1880, an incident occurred which sent him spinning off on a fateful tangent. He was visiting in Canton, which is only about eighteen miles from Ogdensburg. The county fair was being held and he went out to see it—probably to admire the horses that were exhibited. Quite by accident he was introduced to a young woman who was the house guest of a girl he knew. The visitor's name was Eva Adele Caten, and she lived in Gloversville, New York. She was a vivacious girl, with big blue eyes, a pretty face, fine complexion, and wore her clothes with particular grace. She was attracted to the tawny-headed young man, but whatever impression he made upon her was for the time kept strictly to herself. As for Fred Remington, however, it almost immediately became a publicly established fact that no young lady had ever affected him so profoundly. He immediately began a courtship which, in a very short time, took him to Gloversville to ask Eva Caten's father for her hand in marriage. Mr. Lawton Caten, however, was a sensible gentleman who had raised five children and had their future welfare in mind. He gave serious and tolerant consideration to the stability and future prospects of this aspiring son-in-law. Despite the young man's

HARPER'S WEEKLY.

A JOURNAL OF CIVILIZATION.

Vol. XXX.—No. 1516.
Copyright, 1886, by Harper & Brothers.

NEW YORK, SATURDAY, JANUARY 9, 1886.

TEN CENTS A COPY.
$4.00 PER YEAR, IN ADVANCE.

INDIAN SCOUTS ON GERONIMO'S TRAIL

The first picture by Frederic Remington to appear exclusively as his own in any national publication

attractive personality and healthy vigor, he had so far shown no promising signs of the stability suitable for the head of a family. He had failed to finish college—he could not even hold a simple job as a clerk—and more than one unkind person had predicted that he would never amount to anything. Mr. Caten rejected his request for the hand of his daughter in marriage.

It was a bitter blow for Frederic. Under his stalwart appearance he had the sensitive nature of a dreamer. Like many young men who have paid little attention to girls, when he found the right one he gave his whole heart not lightly but completely. The hurt to his pride, too, was deep and cutting. It may have brought him to a realization of his own shortcomings. He made up his mind to leave the part of the world where he had suffered such a staggering rebuff and where Eva's presence made her unattainability even more painful—he would go West, make his fortune in short order, and return to confound her father by his success. Then they would marry and all would be well. He set out toward the Mississippi and the wild land beyond with the declared intention of "becoming a millionaire." He had a liking for the fine things that money could provide. He had also learned that the earning of any great sum, starting as a clerk or apprentice in any business he knew, was far too slow and irksome a process for his peculiar nature. Many another young and adventurous spirit had gone West and found quick fortune. If others could, why not Fred Remington?

So it was not as an artist that Frederic turned to the West, but as an impatient and rather reckless youth who saw in the wild lands beyond the Mississippi a place where quick fortune waited to be plucked by eager hands.

CHAPTER IV

College Boy to Cowboy

ONLY four years before Remington first saw the plains and prairies that he was to make peculiarly his own, General Custer and over two hundred of his men had met death fighting the Sioux. Six years would elapse before Geronimo, the wily Apache leader, allowed the United States Army to capture him; and ten before the clever Medicine Chief of the Sioux, Sitting Bull, was killed resisting arrest. Might was right and brute strength the standard of excellence in an untamed land where renegade redskin bands roamed armed with Winchesters instead of bows and arrows; where the train robber and the all-around "bad man" were commonplace; and trappers, hunters and squaw-owning frontiersmen could and did still find plenty of wilderness into which to retreat before the obnoxious march of civilization. The West was still the land of the riders of the open cattle range and of the war trail.

To Frederic Remington, the nineteen-year-old Easterner, the raw and rugged life of the West seemed to be the answer to his restless desire—an engrossing romance, the pages of which he could hardly read and turn fast enough. Already an excellent rider and judge of horseflesh, he quickly learned to throw a lariat with the skill of a trained cowboy and to handle a six-gun like a master. His fists were powerful weapons and he never feared or avoided a fight. All these were essential equipment for good health and good standing, but Frederic brought more to the West—he brought the artist's observant eye, an insatiable curiosity, a boundless interest in people and places. He wandered through the Dakotas, Montana, Wyoming, Kansas and the territories of states still unnamed. He sought out the roughest and most exciting parts of the country, and the roughest and most colorful of the people who gave the country its character. All his restless energy now concentrated on seeing into the lives, the thoughts and purposes of the people with whom he lived and worked as a hired cowboy or riding with the wagon trains across plains and desert and through the passes of the Rockies. He

33

spent much time around the encampments of the various Indian tribes and learned to know one from the other. He took part in punitive expeditions against renegade Indians and whites. Everything that made up the daily lives of both Western white and red men—their horses, their intimate customs and private lore, their costumes and even their attitudes toward one another—he came to know as he had once known the little village of Canton.

Not only did Remington quickly adopt the life of the West and accustom himself to its ways, but with equal promptness he caught the inspiration which was to lead him to his career. The almost casual way in which his intense absorption in Western places and people became the main purpose of his life can best be told in his own words:

"Evening overtook me one night in Montana and I by good luck made the camp-fire of an old wagon freighter who shared his bacon and coffee with me. I was 19 years of age and he was a very old man. Over the pipes it developed that he was born in western New York and had gone West at an early age. His West was Iowa. Thence during his long life he had followed the receding frontiers, always further and further West.

" 'And now,' said he, 'there is no more West. In a few years the railroad will come along the Yellowstone and a poor man cannot make an honest living at all.'

"There he was, my friend of the open, sleeping in a blanket on the ground (it snowed that night), eating his villainies out of a frying pan, wearing a cotton shirt open at the throat, and hunting horses through the bleak hills before daylight; and all for enough money to mend harness and buy wagon grease. He had his point of view and he made a new one for me.

"The old man had closed my very entrancing book almost at the first chapter. I knew the railroad was coming. I saw men already swarming into the land. I knew the derby hat, the smoking chimneys, the cord-binder, and the thirty-day note were upon us in a restless surge. I knew the wild riders and the vacant land were about to vanish forever—and the more I considered the subject, the bigger the *forever* loomed.

"Without knowing exactly how to do it, I began to try to record some facts around me, and the more I looked the more the panorama unfolded. Youth is never appalled by the insistent demands of a great profession, because it is mostly unconscious of their existence. Time unfolds these abruptly enough. Art is a she-devil of a mistress, and, if at times in earlier days she would not even stoop to my way of thinking, I have persevered and will so continue. Some day, who knows, she may let me tell you some of my secrets. Meanwhile be patient, and if the recording of a day which is past infringes upon the increasing interest in the present, be assured there are those who will set this down in turn and everything will be right in the end. Besides, artists must follow their own inclinations unreservedly. It's more a matter of heart than head, with nothing perfunctory about it. I saw the living, breathing end of three

34

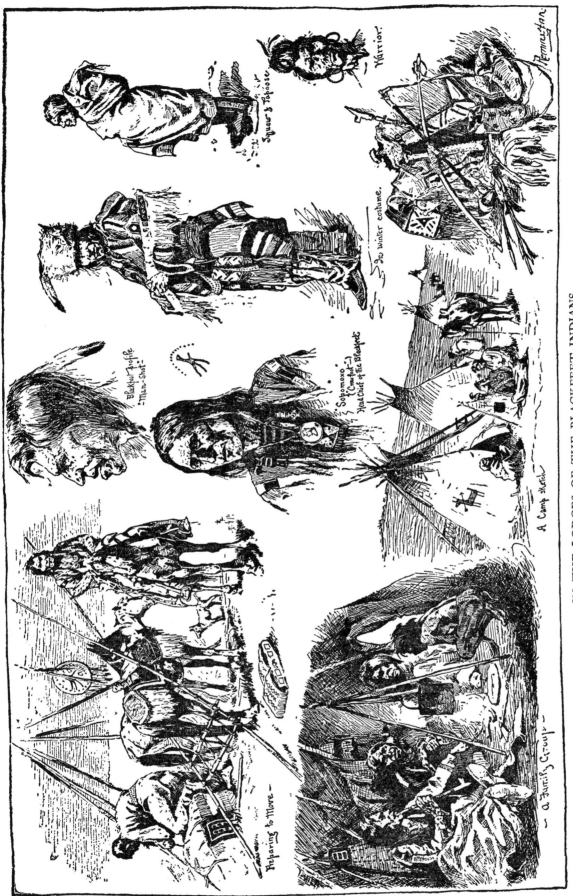

IN THE LODGES OF THE BLACKFEET INDIANS
Harper's Weekly, July 23, 1887

American centuries of smoke and dust and sweat; and I now see quite another thing where it all took place . . . but it does not appeal to me."*

Writing some twenty-five years after the event, Remington not unnaturally recollected the establishment of his goal as considerably more clean-cut than it actually had been. He was not yet through with cross-purposes and uncertainties, though there is probably no doubt that he began to work seriously at about this time.

That he had his sights set, more or less seriously, on an artistic career is pretty well substantiated by a picture which appeared in *Harper's Weekly* on February 25, 1882. It bore the title "Cow-boys of Arizona—Roused by a Scout" and the credit line reads, "Drawn by W. A. Rogers from a Sketch by Frederic Remington." The story of how that full-page picture got into the leading magazine of the day was told years later when Remington and Rogers met. Called into the editor's office, Rogers had been handed a piece of rather crumpled ordinary wrapping paper which had been folded and sent through the mail in a letter envelope. On it was drawn a sketch depicting a group of Western cowboys being routed out of their saddle blankets on the open ground by a mounted confederate who had ridden in to warn them of approaching danger. The sketch was crude and of course the signature of Frederic Remington meant nothing more than a name—but the picture had something which caused the editor to give it to Rogers, a staff man, to be re-drawn for publication. Remington had sent it from Wyoming.

"I remember with how much pleasure I made a drawing on wood for that little sketch," Rogers reminisced to Remington, "and I recall having admired it greatly. But I had forgotten the entire circumstances long before the name of Frederic Remington meant anything to me."

"Yes," said Remington, "it was you who introduced me to the public. That was my first appearance and I was mighty glad I fell into the hands of an artist who knew a cowboy saddle and a Western horse."†

Perhaps his money was beginning to run out or perhaps his restlessness had been assuaged by the months of foot-loose wandering; at any rate he made an attempt to settle down near Kansas City, in the little town of Peabody, Kansas, where he tried his hand at ranching and raising mules. He was thoroughly familiar with Kansas City, a rowdy, booming metropolis of about seventy-five thousand, an important cattle center, abounding with gambling and drinking places, where questionable characters from remote corners of the West rubbed elbows with tenderfoot Easterners. Fred got along with all kinds; he drank all night with cowboys and old-timers at Gaston's or the Pacific or Billy Christie's, and he was on easy terms with the more respectable element which included such men as John Mulvaney, painter of the famous "Custer's

* "A Few Words from Mr. Remington," *Collier's Weekly*, Mar. 18, 1905.
† Rogers, W. A., *A World Worth While*, Harper & Bros., 1922.

Last Stand," George Gaston, an ex-Bavarian colonel who spoke five languages and was an acknowledged connoisseur of music, art and roast beef; and Charlie Bennett, the sheriff who tended bar at Bishop & Christie's. Al Hatch, who ran the roadhouse at the edge of town, was a particular friend who sometime later remarked that "if Fred hadn't gone in for art, he could have made a great prize fighter. Not a bully, mind you, but a very nervy kid, with bull strength. I stayed sorry for two weeks, because I made the mistake of putting the gloves on with him."

He became a familiar sight, riding out Independence Avenue beyond the edge of town, with a rope trailing behind his spirited horse. Many a morning at daybreak, after an all-night round of the gathering places, he would go out into the country just for the sheer joy of it—and lasso sunflowers for practice and diversion. To none of those who knew him at that time was he Frederic Remington the artist—just a husky young fellow with sufficient means to scorn routine work and a deep desire to get all out of life that life was willing to let him have.

On December 29, 1883, Remington wrote to an old friend, Arthur Merkly, stating that he was "trying to sell here and go somewhere else . . . and when I get my money out of this scheme I am going further West . . . and there tackle some business. I don't care whether it is stock, Mercantile—either hardware or Whiskey—or anything else. I should like nothing better in the world than to find a partner in whom I had confidence and who had a little money. You are acquainted with the hardware biz. I believe. Why not start a hardware ranch out West?"

A photograph taken of him at about this time shows a blondish young man with an unaggressive moustache, a heavy chin, rather sensitive mouth, a prominent nose and well-shaped eyes. He was heavy-set, not tall but powerful, and never went in for eccentricities of dress, either Western or Bohemian. He had, as a matter of fact, an impelling taste for the good things of life. If he could have discovered some way of making money, which did not tie him down to one place or make it impossible to paint and sketch as much as he wanted, he would undoubtedly have leaped at the chance. Nor was Eva forgotten.

In the early spring of 1884 Remington disposed of his ranch, which had been, if not an outright failure, at least far from the gold mine he hoped for, and once more headed westward, planning to go deep into the Southwest and over into Old Mexico.

Remington had already seen far more of the West than most men who had spent a far longer period beyond the Mississippi. Most of his time had been spent in seeking out the places which were the least affected by the steady westward march of civilization. He had traveled the routes of the Oregon Trail, the Santa Fe Trail and the less-known trails pioneered by such men as Kit Carson, Jedediah Smith and many another pioneer who led the way to the taming of the vast West. He had ridden, camped, hunted and come to know practically every section, Indian tribe and type of white man from the Bad Lands to the Rockies and from the Canadian Border to the Rio Grande.

Becoming an artist had been a rather vague sort of dream, which continued to follow him as persistently as his shadow. This trip to the Southwest in the spring of 1884 was the first on which he devoted any really serious effort to making sketches in the field, which he might sell or could later use as the basis for more finished pictures.

He went among the Cheyennes and the Comanches in Indian Territory, and the Apaches in Arizona, for the definite purpose of making drawings of these Indians just as he found them; and he went into Mexico to hunt with the *vaqueros*, as well as to sketch.

Remington still had enough money left to permit his enjoying modest independence. If he saw a horse that particularly appealed to him, and the owner was disposed to part with the animal, he could buy it and usually did; and he spent a good deal of money purchasing or trading for choice articles of Indian and cowboy adornment, such as finely beaded buckskin garments, ceremonial dance paraphernalia, silver-decorated horse trappings and other such Western accoutrements in which he always had an intense interest as a collector.

But all this was, for the moment, getting him nowhere in particular. What money he had left would run out in the not very distant future; and matrimonial ideas had been occupying an increasingly important part in his thoughts.

CHAPTER V

A Bride Goes West

WHEN Fred returned to Kansas City after a few months, he had a thick portfolio of sketches and a measure of assurance in his own ability. He took a little house in the residential district of Kansas City, set himself to working up his sketches, and that summer made his first sales. The paintings told stories, they were realistic, they were truthful. They were not particularly beautiful or technically excellent, but they had something which strongly appealed to the cowboys and all those who knew the men of the plains and the horses they rode. To both white men and red men they represented something that was a part of their own lives; the horses were portraits of the animals they rode; the decorated leggings and beaded moccasins had the appearance of the things their squaws made; and the backgrounds were out of their own recollections.

Some of the pictures were purchased by William W. Findlay, who was proprietor of a Kansas City store that handled pictures. He paid Remington as much as one hundred dollars for some of his paintings. In fact, it is reasonable to suspect that William W. Findlay had more faith in the artistic future of this sturdy young man, back in those early 80's, than Fred Remington himself. As evidence of Findlay's good judgment and sound business acumen, the firm which he established is still enjoying more than ordinary prosperity under his name. Many years later, the son of the founder paid seven thousand five hundred dollars for one of Remington's early pictures which in 1888 his father had purchased for two hundred and seventy-five dollars; and it was to be the lot of the grandson of William W. Findlay, three score years later, to pay the highest price ever realized from a Remington painting.

That same summer of 1884 he was offered a business opportunity which seemed the answer to every problem. A third interest and silent partner in one of Kansas City's most prosperous emporiums that was doing a thriving business catering to thirsty cowboys was surely a wise investment even though it took nearly all his remaining capital. He would have, he thought, a steady income making it possible to roam as he willed, to paint and draw to his heart's content. And he could marry. It was not the fortune he had dreamed of, but it was good enough and he began making plans to return to Gloversville where Eva, he knew from her letters, still waited for him. With his new self-confidence he was sure he could soften Mr. Caten's heart.

In the midst of his planning to go East, his saloon moved to bigger and better quarters on a more prosperous street and the proprietors are reported to have informed the silent partner that, according to their way of figuring, he had no further interest or equity in the concern. Fred was apparently the victim of a trick not uncommon among unscrupulous frontier businessmen, and, as he had no legal receipt or security for his investment, his one-third interest vanished like the smoke from the top of an Indian tepee.

His reaction was immediate and violent. With his six-gun in hand and blood in his eye, he went on a search for the culprit to even up the score; and only the intervention of a friend persuaded him that gunplay was not a satisfactory way to settle the matter. Civilized methods were no more effective. as it proved, for Remington never recovered a penny of his money.

It was a staggering setback, but he made up his mind nothing would stop him now and somehow managed to scrape together enough money to get to Gloversville. His determination must have impressed Mr. Caten favorably, for this time his request was granted. On October 1, 1884, Eva Caten became Mrs. Frederic Remington in a quiet ceremony at her father's home.

Very shortly afterward he took his attractive bride proudly back to Kansas City where "Missie," as he called her, settled into the little house he had lived in since his return from the Southwest. For some time they were as happy as young people should be, who are together at last after a long separation.

But then things began to go badly. Kansas City, at the edge of the wild country of Indians and cowboys and the open range, was a tough morsel for a gently bred girl to assimilate. It was all strange and a little frightening and very lonely. And they were poor. Frederic's inheritance had vanished and painting brought in slim pickings.

Striving for that recognition which might give him even so narrow a toe hold in the field of artistic endeavor and economic security, Remington continued to send pictures back East in search of publication. Just how many such pictures he sent, or to how many magazines they were submitted, is not known. The results, however, are restricted to a single additional illustration published in *Harper's Weekly*, in the issue of March 28, 1885. "Ejecting an 'Oklahoma Boomer' " was used on the cover of the magazine, carrying the credit line, "Drawn by T. de Thulstrup from a Sketch by Frederic Remington." Encouraging though this may have been, it fell a long way short of providing the necessities of life for Remington and his newly acquired bride.

40

THE OLD TRAPPER
Century, October 1888

THE FIRST OF THE RACE
Century, January 1889

LADRONE
Century, September 1891

A PULL AT THE CANTEEN
Century, April 1889

At last the young couple were faced with a situation which called for drastic measures. Should he get some routine job and give up the dream of living as an artist? Or was there another path that might, if they had sufficient courage and faith in one another, lead them safely through this morass?

It must have been a hard decision to make, for they were much in love; but Frederic was by now realistic enough about himself to recognize the dangers lurking behind the smooth façade of a regular job and money in the bank; he would never be happy, nor successful as both he and Eva visualized success for him; and if he were miserable and discontented Eva would be, too. Better swallow their pride now, they thought, and hope that the new start would be the right one.

Less than a year after she left Gloversville with the good wishes of her family and friends ringing in her ears, Eva returned East to wait again. Frederic's mother hurried out to Kansas City, but her efforts to turn him the way she thought he ought to go were unavailing; he and his wife had made their choice and Mrs. Remington was forced to acknowledge that her boy was now a man and to leave him to work out his own salvation.

The story of how Fred Remington left their town is still told by some of the older residents of Kansas City. He was standing on a street corner near the center of the little Western metropolis, when a house painter by the name of "Shorty" Reason drove by in a spring wagon drawn by a tough gray mare.

"Want to sell that mare?" called Remington.

"Nope," replied Shorty, who was wise in the ways of horse trading. But he stopped the horse.

"Is she good under the saddle?" inquired Remington, knowing she was.

"Try her for yourself," countered Shorty.

In the center of Kansas City, the mare was unhitched; a borrowed saddle was cinched onto her; and Remington swung up astride to try her. They finally agreed on a price of fifty dollars.

At daybreak the next morning Fred Remington rode out of town. He went alone. He had in his pockets practically everything he owned in the way of worldly possessions. He was headed again for the wild country of the far Southwest.

CHAPTER VI

Among Apaches and Comanches

FRED joined a couple of prospectors in Arizona Territory for a prospecting expedition on the south side of the Pinal Range, an area in which the Apache leader, Geronimo, and his followers were reported active in their favorite avocations of ambush, murder and massacre. The United States Army was making a desperate effort to keep the situation under control without causing a general uprising among the Apaches, at the cost of many casualties and much embarrassment. During the time Remington was camped in the Pinal Range, Captain Emmet Crawford of the Third Cavalry under General Crook, had trailed a large band for many days in the same vicinity, overtaking them finally in a running battle with casualties on both sides. Another band called the "Bloody Eleven" was known to have killed forty-eight white men near by, within four weeks. The prospectors were alert enough to their danger, but were not unduly affected by it, as the account of that part of the trip which Remington wrote a few years later would seem to prove:

"We were seated beside our little cooking fire about 9 o'clock in the evening, engaged in smoking and drowsily discussing the celerity of movement displayed by Geronimo. . . . Conversation lapsed at last and puffing our pipes and lying stretched on our backs we looked up into the dark branches of the trees above . . . when I felt moved to sit up.

"My breath went with the look I gave; for, to my unbounded astonishment and consternation, there sat three Apaches on the opposite side of our fire, with their rifles across their laps. My comrades also saw them; and, old, hardened frontiersmen that they were, they positively gasped in amazement.

" 'Heap hungry,' ejaculated one of the savage apparitions, and again relapsed into silence.

"As we were not familiar with the personal appearance of Mr. Geronimo's countenance, we thought we could see the old villain's features in our interlocutor's, and we began to get our artillery into shape for use.

"The savages, in an apparent effort to allay the disturbance which they had very plainly created, now explained:

" 'We White Mountain. No want fight—want flour.'

"They got the flour in generous quantities, it is needless to add; and although we had previously been very sleepy, we now sat up and entertained our self-invited guests until they condescended to stretch themselves out and go to sleep. We pretended to do the same. During that night, however, I never closed my eyes; but watched and listened, momentarily expecting to see more visitors come gliding out of the darkness. I should not have been surprised even to see an Apache drop from a branch above me.

"Morning finally came; and they left us, with a blessing couched in the style of forcible speech that my Rocky Mountain friends affected on unusual occasions.

"I mused over the occurrence. For a while it brought no more serious consequences than the loss of some odd pounds of bacon and flour, yet there was a warning in the way those Apaches could usurp the prerogatives of ghosts."*

Prospecting failed to yield either profit or encouragement. By the time hot summer had come to scorch the sands and make the canyons like humid bake-ovens, he abandoned the unsatisfying task of digging among the rocky cliffs in search of a phantom fortune. There were other pursuits to which he might have turned for occupation; but without capital, these offered little more than routine jobs as a paid employee. After wandering around rather aimlessly for some time, he found himself on Arizona's San Carlos Reservation. This was a vast tract of desert and mountain land on the Gila River, given over as a place on which to herd the Apache Indians in an attempt to keep them under control.

"I arrived at this place one evening after a hot and tiresome march in company with a cavalry command. I found a good bunk in the tent of an Army officer whose heart went out to the man in search of the picturesque, and I was invited to destroy my rations that evening at the long table of the officers' mess.

"On the following morning I got out my sketch-book, and taking my host into my confidence I explained my plans for action. The captain abruptly discontinued brushing his hair and looked at me with a humorous twinkle in his eye. 'Young man,' he said, 'if you desire to wear a long, gray beard you must make away with the idea that you are in Venice.'

"I remembered that the year before a Blackfoot on the Bow River had shown a desire to tomahawk me because I was endeavoring to immortalize him. After a long and tedious course of diplomacy it is at times possible to get one of these people to gaze in a defiant and fearful way into the eye of a camera; but to stand still until a

* "On the Indian Reservation," Frederic Remington, *Century Magazine*, July 1889.

SKETCH IN THE SOLDIER CLAN DANCE
Harper's Monthly, December 1891

THROWING THE SNOW SNAKE
Harper's Monthly, December 1891.

INDIAN BOYS RUNNING A FOOT RACE
Harper's Monthly, December 1891

man draws his picture on paper or canvas is a proposition which no Apache will entertain for a moment.

"With the help of two officers, who stood up close to me, I was enabled to make rapid sketches of the scenes and people; but my manner at last aroused suspicion and my game would vanish like a covey of quail.

"From the parade in front of our tent I could see the long lines of horses, mules and burros trooping into the agency from all quarters. Here was my feast. Ordinarily the Indians are scattered for forty miles in every direction; but this was ration-day and they were all together.

"Hundreds of ponies, caparisoned in all sorts of fantastic ways, were standing around. Young girls of the San Carlos tribe flitted about, attracting my attention by the queer ornaments which, in token of their virginity, they wear in their hair. Tall Yuma bucks galloped past with their long hair flying out behind. The squaws crowded around the exit and received the great chunks of beef which a native butcher threw to them. Indian scouts in military coats and armed with rifles stood about to preserve order. Groups of old women sat on the hot ground and gossiped. An old chief, with a very respectable adipose under his cartridge-belt, galloped up. . . .

"We strolled among the horses and mules. They would let me sketch them, though I thought the half-wild beasts also shrunk away from the baleful gaze of the white man with his pencil and bit of paper. Broncos, mules and burros stood about, with bags of flour tied on their saddles and great chunks of meat dripping blood over their unkempt sides. These woe-begone beasts find scant pasture in their desert home and are banged about by their savage masters until ever-present evils triumph over equine philosophy. Fine navy blankets and articles of Mexican manufacture were stretched over some of the saddles, the latter probably obtained in a manner not countenanced by international law.

"The sun sinks behind the distant Sierras and the beautiful quiet tones of the after glow spread over the fields and the water; and as I stand there watching the scene I can almost imagine that I see Millet's peasants—but, alas! I know too well the difference. . . .

"Leaving the troopers about their fires, we take our way in company with an old Government Indian scout to his own *jicail*. The frugal evening meal was soon disposed of, and taking our cigarettes we sat on the bluffs and smoked.

"It grew dark, and we forbore to talk. Presently, as though to complete the strangeness of the situation, the measured '*thump, thump, thump*' of the tom-tom came from the vicinity of a fire some short distance away. One wild voice raised itself in strange discordant sounds, dropped low, and then rose again, swelling into shrill yelps, in which others joined. We listened—and the wild sounds to our accustomed ears became almost tuneful and harmonious. We drew nearer, and by the little flicker-

46

ing light of the fire discerned half-naked forms huddled with uplifted faces in a small circle around the tom-tom. The fire cut queer lights on their rugged outlines; the waves of sound rose and fell; and the 'thump, thump, thump, thump' of the tom-tom kept a binding time. We grew in sympathy with the strange concert, and sat down some distance off and listened for hours. It was more enjoyable in its way than any trained chorus I have ever heard."*

From the San Carlos and the burning sands of Arizona Territory, Remington wandered into the grassy ranges of Texas. There, at the little town of Henriette, he struck up a friendship with a Texas cowboy with whom he rode northward through the Indian Territory. "He was a good fellow and full of interest," Remington reported later; "had made the Montana Trail three times with the Hash Knife outfit; and was full of quaint expressions peculiar to Western Americans. He gave me volumes of information concerning Comanches and Indians in general."*

He and the cowboy roved on horseback across the rolling plains of northern Texas until they came to the Red River and fording it they entered Indian Territory. In due course they reached Fort Sill, one of the principal military strongholds of the area as well as reservation headquarters for the Comanche Indians. Here the artist and cowboy parted company and Remington began a somewhat similar friendship with the official Comanche interpreter, Horace P. Jones. During the thirty-one years Jones had lived with the Comanche tribe he had garnered much out-of-the-way knowledge about Comanches and Indians in general; he was a recognized authority and Remington profited by the association.

Fred liked being among the Comanches particularly, because of their intelligent handling and breeding of horses. "They apply an amount of good sense to their handling of horses which I have never seen among Indians elsewhere," he wrote. "They breed intelligently and produce some of the most beautiful 'painted' ponies imaginable. They take good care of them, and in buying and selling have no lesson to learn from Yankee horse-traders." But he knew Indians too well to have illusions about them. "Bidding adieu to my friends at Fort Sill," he commented regarding the termination of this experience, "I pulled out for Anadarko on the Washita . . . and I thought then, that the good white men who would undertake to make Christian gentlemen and honest tillers of the soil out of this raw human material, would be contracting for a job to subvert the process of nature."*

* "On the Indian Reservation," Frederic Remington, Century Magazine, July 1889.

CHAPTER VII

Struggles to Succeed

ORTUNE continued elusive as ever. Remington was not one of the favored who "struck it rich." The earth failed to inform him of her gold, nor did the young man's beloved West spread her other obvious riches at his unquiet feet. He had tried very hard, but he had to all evident appearances failed quite miserably. All that he seemed to have gained was an acute case of homesickness for Missie and an increased desire to draw and paint the colorful passing parade of the wild Western scene.

He came back to Kansas City at the end of the summer of 1885, with a crudely improvised portfolio jammed with sketches and drawings which he had made in the camps and along the trails he had traveled. Financially, he was as destitute and barren as the driest alkali arroyo he had seen in all his wanderings, but he now determined to go to New York in the hope of selling some of his pictures. There seemed no other avenue open to him. Just how he was to get back East, however, presented a problem of no small dimensions. Of course, there were friends in Kansas City who would lend him money and one story indicates that this is what happened. The other version is more colorful, though not contradictory of the first, and was told by J. Henry Harper in *The House of Harper*, his history of the publishing firm which started Remington on the road to success and, over a period of time, used more of his work than any other publisher:

"When the late Frederic Remington first appeared in our office he looked like a cowboy just off a ranch, which, in fact, was the case. The sketches he brought with him were very crude but they had all the ring of new and live material. In the course of conversation with him he told me that his ranch life had proved an utter failure and that he had recently found himself stranded in a small western town with but a quarter of a dollar in his pockets. He was anxious to get to New York, but was at a loss to conceive where the funds were to come from to pay his carfare over. As he entered an unprepossessing little inn in the evening he noticed that there was a game of poker in progress in the open bar-room, and he took the situation in at a glance: two professional gamblers were plucking a man who looked like an Eastern drummer. Remington watched the players for a few minutes and then suggested to the commercial traveler that he had better stop and go to bed. The savage looks of the two gamblers put Remington on his guard and he whipped out his gun, told the card-sharps to hold up their hands and covered his retreat until he and his befriended companion were safe in the man's bedroom and had locked and barricaded the door. Remington, anticipating further trouble, sat with his gun ready all night, and when he heard stealthy footsteps outside their door, several hours later, he gave the rustlers clear evidence that he was awake and ready for action. Remington's new-found friend was overwhelming in his gratitude and begged to know how he could recompense Remington for his timely assistance. Remington said that he desired to go to New York, but lacked the required funds. The upshot was that his new acquaintance was also on his way to the same city and invited Remington to accompany him at his expense."

According to his own story, Fred arrived in New York with a total capital of three dollars. Eva came down from Gloversville to join him and the reunion was a happy one though the future looked as cloudy as on the day he stood on the station platform waving her goodbye in Kansas City. Once again he faced the problem of providing for them both, and once again his hands were almost empty. Luckily they could live with friends, the Benjamin W. Wilsons, who had a home on Ross Street in Brooklyn, and Frederic set out to sell his pictures of cowboys and Indians.

Although he did not realize it at first, the subject matter of his work was unpopular among magazine editors in that winter of 1885-1886. The United States was still a young and debtor nation, on the threshold of a great industrial development. Vast financial credits and investments were needed to carry through the extensive programs of railroads, mines, foundries, factories, banks and national expansion in many other economic fields. Our financiers and politicians, looking to European countries for assistance, were supersensitive about such barbarisms as Indians and our turbulent pioneering tradition. There were already too many people in London, Paris and Berlin who seriously believed that painted wild Indians were an everyday menace to life even along Broadway, and our national policy makers were bent on creating the impression, both abroad and in the Eastern states, that all was very calm and civilized in our rich and fertile great West. Pictures of fat hogs and contented cows, happy homesteaders with children around them, smiling and dirty-faced miners and carloads of grain, were far more attractive to the eye of the editor than drawings of gallant soldiers and buckskin-clad pioneers being killed by half-naked Indians. A

49

vastly more experienced artist than young Frederic Remington would have found this attitude an almost impossible hurdle to leap.

He plodded doggedly through the streets of New York, so different from the free wild places that he loved, from one publication office to another—only to meet with cold indifference. There was no money to waste on hansom cabs and even the few pennies for riding on a horse-drawn trolley were looked at twice. Many times he must have thought longingly of the days when his own horse was as much a part of him as his feet. But no matter how many editors he managed to see, his portfolio remained discouragingly full. Even without a wife to support, he could not go on indefinitely. He took a job as a clerk, but could not stand it more than a day. Then his uncle, William Remington, came to the rescue by lending him enough money to try a little longer. With this money he went to classes at the Art Students League where he worked sincerely to improve his knowledge of techniques, and where he met other artists, among them A. B. Frost, E. W. Kemble and others whose work as illustrators and artists was to bring them fame and money; but Fred Remington could not spend much time learning. Very soon the pressure to earn started him off again trying to sell.

Finally, Henry Mills Alden, Art Editor of *Harper's Weekly*, who had bought those two first rough sketches, became interested; and Remington's first picture to be published under his name alone appeared as a full-page cover illustration in *Harper's Weekly* in the issue of January 9, 1886. It was titled "The Apache War—Indian Scouts on Geronimo's Trail." This was really the beginning. Afterward Remington pictures began appearing with steadily increasing regularity in this important national weekly.

Although most other editors continued to turn a cold shoulder, the appearance of his work in America's most popular weekly could not be without its effect. In the year 1886, he illustrated a story by Frances C. Baylor for *St. Nicholas* with two drawings which appeared later in the published book, *Juan and Juanita*; and he got his toe securely inside the door of *Outing Magazine*—just how can best be told by quoting from the autobiography of the man who was the owner and editor at the time:

"One day at the *Outing* office I was hard at work making up a forthcoming number. I was interrupted by a vast portfolio in the hands of some intruding one. Of course, I knew that this meant looking at some drawings and probably turning away some artist who needed money and needed still more of the qualities to make success. Feeling cross and weary, I did not even look up at the huge visitor, but held out a hand for the drawings. He pushed one at me, and it was as though he had given me an electric shock. Here was the real thing, the unspoiled native genius dealing with Mexican ponies, cowboys, cactus, lariats and sombreros. No stage heroes these; no careful pomaded hair and neatly tied cravats; these were the men of the real rodeo, parched in alkali dust, blinking out from barely opened eyes under the furious rays of

"I TOOK YE FOR AN INJIN"
Century, November 1890

AMERICAN, MEXICAN AND FRENCH PIONEER TYPES
Century, March 1891

the Arizona sun. I had been there and my innermost corpuscle vibrated at the truth before me. I looked at the signature . . . Remington.

" 'It's an odd coincidence, I had a classmate at Yale . . .' I said to him. But before I could add another word, out he roared: 'Hell, Big, is that you?' And so it was."*

The editor was Poultney Bigelow, Remington's former Art School classmate at Yale.

"He had turned himself into a cowboy," Bigelow goes on, "and I had become a slave to a desk. We embraced; we made so much noise that my colleagues in the outer office feared that a fight was on. I introduced all present and then pulled from the pigeon-holes every manuscript likely to interest such a pencil. Anything that might serve as an excuse for introducing horses, cowboys, army types. Nearly every great magazine in New York had turned him away from the desk of the so-called art editor because none of their orthodox picture buyers could see anything good in a horse that had not been groomed or a soldier in shirt sleeves. But genius was in the rough drawings and I loved them for their roughness. Of course, I bought all he had in his portfolio, and I loaded him with orders likely to keep him in every number of the magazine for two or three years."*

Bigelow had overestimated very little. Remington first appeared in *Outing* in December 1886 and during the following year there were only two issues in which his work was not included, and frequently he illustrated more than one article in the same number. The first assignment was to illustrate a series of articles called "After Geronimo" by Lieutenant John Bigelow, for which no better man could possibly have been found. His pen-and-ink sketches of Tenth Cavalry types and action scenes during the pursuit of the Apache renegades were alive with Remington's own memories of the not so distant days when he had gone prospecting under Geronimo's very nose—a bit of good luck for artist, author and editor.

The eventful year 1886 had also seen the first Remington illustrations published in a book. *Mexico of Today* by Solomon Buckley Griffin contains two of Remington's pen-and-ink drawings and, though the author is forgotten, his book is a collector's item today because of the illustrations.

Remington was as steadfast in his determination to restrict his work to the theme of the Old West as he was to do the best work of which he was capable. He brought to his work qualities of almost incredible industry and perseverance, though the conditions under which he labored were difficult those first years. He and Eva were still boarding with the Wilsons in Brooklyn, and he had only a makeshift place which he used as a studio. During his first winter in New York he also suffered a severe attack of rheumatism in his arm, probably the result of the many nights he had slept on the

* Poultney Bigelow, *Seventy Summers*.

ground in damp blankets. Hard work and fixity of purpose may not be rewarded as often in real life as in story books, but in Remington's case recognition of his ability was already on the way in such measure as to compensate for all the struggle it had cost.

In 1887 Remington had one of his paintings, "The Flag of Truce in the Indian Wars," accepted for hanging in the Annual Exhibition of the American Water Color Society; and that same year another of his paintings, "The Courier's Nap on the Trail," was hung in the Annual Exhibition of the National Academy of Design.

The following year another of his pictures, "Arrest of a Blackfoot Murderer" was included in the Annual Exhibition of the American Water Color Society; and his "Return of a Blackfoot War Party" was the winner of both the Hallgarten and the Clarke prizes in the Sixty-third Annual Exhibition of the National Academy. Nor were these all of the honors bestowed upon this new artist. He had two additional paintings hung in the Autumn Exhibition of the National Academy, in addition to which, during the year 1888, he had fifty-four of his pictures reproduced in *Harper's Weekly*, some issues containing as many as thirteen separate sketches; during this year twenty-three were run on a full page or as a double spread; thirty-two additional illustrations appeared in *Outing*; twenty-seven in *Youth's Companion*; sixty-four in *Century Magazine*; and orders for more work were piling up. The *Century* illustrations began with those for a series of articles by another Old West enthusiast, Theodore Roosevelt, which were published in book form later that year under the title *Ranch Life and the Hunting Trail*, with ninety-nine Remington drawings. The book was a success, establishing Roosevelt as a writer and Remington as a significant artist of the Western scene. A close frendship began between these two men, which continued until Remington's death, and led to their further collaboration in articles and books. They had met first through their common connection with *Outing Magazine*, for which Roosevelt did some of his first writing; it was his admiration for the Remington illustrations there that prompted him to persuade the editor of *Century* to use that particular artist for his articles on the West.

Not only did the verve and realism of his work attract men who knew the West to Remington; the depth and accuracy of his knowledge and his unbiased understanding of Indian nature, as well as of the life of the Western white man, marked him out as an authority on a subject little known and just then very much in the minds of thoughtful people. The American attitude about the Indian was vacillating among three points of view: The Army's; the frontiersman-pioneer's; and the Eastern philanthropist's. The Army asserted positively that "the only good Indian is a dead Indian." The attitude of the frontiersman and pioneer-settler went far beyond that to covet the (preferably, but not necessarily, dead) Indian's land and everything upon it of any real or imaginary value. The philanthropist, on the other hand, was inspired to play the rôle of good Samaritan to a people who had been grievously wronged.

Americans were beginning to weigh the long and terrible story of Indian brutalities against the equally long and ignominious story of the conqueror's injustice to the Indian. In contrast to horrible accounts of Indian atrocities came the appealing story of *Ramona* which played upon the heartstrings of thousands of readers. With Geronimo only recently incarcerated under Army surveillance, in the devout hope that he would domesticate himself; and Sitting Bull still at large and defying the authorities, the idealists had undertaken a scheme which transferred a few Indians boys and girls from their parents' primitive camps to schools where they were taught English, white man's "morals" and trades. Some of these "educated" Indians had already returned to the campfires of their own people, with their English, their school clothes and their short-cut hair. The results were discouraging—to the "idealists" at least. Most of them did nothing but loaf around the forts and agencies where the white men jabbered pigeon English at them and their untamed cousins sneered. Many went back to their blankets, long hair and filthy tepees; the rest became sullen undesirables in the eyes of both white men and red. It was all very disconcerting.

This was the muddle out of which American public opinion was endeavoring to create an Indian policy that would produce a satisfactory and permanent adjustment between the two races, which future generations might stamp with approval—a hope, it is sad to relate, which has not yet been fulfilled.

Because Remington knew Indians not as a mass but as individuals, he portrayed them without prejudice. He realized that there were many tribal varieties which the average American unthinkingly lumped under the word "Indian." He knew that in each tribe were to be found Geronimos as well as Ramonas, and that the red man's character was as varied as that of the soldiers, frontiersmen, philanthropists and citizens-at-large who pretended to sit in judgment upon a people whom they neither knew nor understood. Both sides in the argument could gain comfort and confirmation from his work, for he drew what he had seen and allowed the results to be their own justification.

Remington soon found the circumstances of his life to be pleasantly reversed. Instead of running around after editors and publishers they began to seek him out. If anything, he worked longer hours and under greater strain, for the sheer quantity of work he was turning out was prodigious. He did not, however, allow the quality of his production to drop off, but bent every nerve to improve it. Both by temperament and force of circumstances he was necessarily almost entirely self-taught, which probably slowed his progress even as it left intact the thing he valued most—his unique individuality.

He rose at six o'clock every morning (a program he followed all his life) to work steadily until the middle of the afternoon. Then he would start off for a long walk or rent a horse from some riding academy for an hour or two; and in the evening he went back to what he had been working on in the morning, planning changes and improvements to be done the next day. It was said of him somewhat later that he was "the most vigorous and busiest artist in America," and certainly only stubborn will power and stern dedication to a high purpose could have enforced so rigorous a schedule.

Now that he was assured of a reasonably steady income, the Remingtons moved from Brooklyn to Manhattan—"Gothum" as Fred liked to call New York City. They established themselves in comparatively pretentious quarters at 360 West 58th Street, in what Fred referred to as "Marlborough Tenement," just off Columbus Circle. Here he improvised a studio in the parlor and surrounded himself with the Indian and cowboy paraphernalia, decorations, curios, guns and other mementos of the West which made famous his later and more spacious studios. This was nearer than Brooklyn to the editorial offices and an even shorter distance to several riding academies where he could rent a horse for an afternoon's ride in Central Park.

Eva's younger sister, Emma, spent a good deal of time with them and found no reason to reverse her original good opinion of her brother-in-law, in spite of his habit of dropping into cowboy vernacular, his frank and profuse profanity, and his deep-rooted dislike of formality.

CHAPTER VIII

Western Americana in Manhattan

A s soon as Frederic had enough money in the bank to tide Eva over until his return, he started West again. This time, however, he went with a new self-assurance and a clear-cut incentive, no casual wanderer but a man of consequence, with letters of introduction explaining that he was on assignment by a national magazine to procure material on the Army and Indians in the Southwest.

He made a tedious and tough trip with a scouting party of the Tenth United States Cavalry from Fort Grant, set among the hot sands of Arizona Territory. The assignment was to check up on some of the more questionable bands of Apaches in the district. This was in the summer of 1888, and even the seasoned soldiers found the expedition unusually trying. Remington wrote that the thermometer was "persistently at 125 degrees F," and that the barrel of his carbine burned his hand. They toiled up over the steep, rocky mountain ridges of the Sierras, "now winding among trees and brush, scrambling up precipitous slopes, picking our way across fields of shattered rock, or steadying our horses over smooth surfaces of boulders," then turning downward "among the masses of rock . . . at an angle of sixty degrees." He sketched constantly—his companions, the country through which they traveled, the many Indian encampments they visited. The miserable Yuma Apaches would come into camp, shake hands gravely with everyone, and then begin the inevitable requests for coffee and flour. The soldiers would gather around the campfire, eating, joking, playing cards or yarning, while Fred made friends with the dirty, ragged Indian children who crept like little wild creatures toward the crackling fire.

The material gathered on that summer trip he used both as artist and author, his articles with illustrations appearing in *Harper's Weekly* and *Century* through the months that followed his return to New York.

One day Miss Caten induced Fred to take her to the Metropolitan Museum of Art—and he rushed her there at a pace which left her gasping. Once arrived at the sprawling red-brick building, she imagined she would be allowed to choose her own gait and gaze leisurely at the paintings. However, her unconventional brother-in-law had no such intention. He hurried her through galleries and corridors, without glancing to one side or the other, until they stood before Jean Meissonier's painting, "Friedland, 1807," in which the magnificently drawn horses are conspicuous. He said, as Miss Caten reports, "This is the only picture in this whole museum that's worth looking at!" Whereupon he dragged her away and the next thing she knew they were walking briskly homeward through the Park.

Beyond the important fact that New York as the nation's center of publishing activities afforded him the means to make a living by doing what he wanted to do, he had little use for the glittering city of "Gothum." Smoky, soot-filled air filtering through streets littered with trash, papers and, all too often, garbage were poor substitutes for the clean prairie winds. Nor was a sedate trot through the forlorn, untended woods and fields of Central Park a satisfactory exchange for a wild gallop on a wilder bronco across the Western plains. People, however, were people and usually therefore friends. Remington liked men who were fearlessly themselves, whether cowboys, Indians, frontier riffraff, or celebrities. For celebrities as such he had small fondness, but he found many who spoke his own language and between Remington and such men as Theodore Roosevelt, Rudyard Kipling, Owen Wister and Augustus Thomas there grew up genuine friendships. Despite the long hours he put in at work in his studio, there was somehow always time for good talks over a bottle, for evenings of conviviality with chosen cronies that ended only as gray dawn crept through the man-made canyons of Manhattan.

Friendship was a long-term affair with Fred Remington. The men he had known when they were boys together in Canton and Ogdensburg, his classmates at Yale, many who had been fellow-students during his brief time at the Art Students League, added their number to the wide circle to whom he could say, as he wrote once to one of them, "come up here and smoke my cigars and drink my rum and eat my grub and you're always welcome. . . ."

William A. Poste, a boyhood friend of Canton days, was giving a formal dinner party for a group of friends at a New York hotel, to which Remington was invited. Since the guests were expected to appear in full dress, Mr. Poste so informed him in the letter of invitation. Remington's letter of acknowledgment was as follows:

MINE HOST—That dress coat proposition is one of the most low-down tricks which a white man could resort to. Of course it is plain enough that you want to economize, well knowing that I have outgrown my dress suit which is now so tight that I cannot take breath, let alone eat in it. But patiently I take my medicine. Order one French chop and an after-dinner coffee—that will be all right if I let out the top button.

This was at the time when the Remingtons were still living on 58th Street in Marlborough Tenement; and when Fred arrived for the party he asked a hotel attendant to announce to Mr. Poste that the "Duke of Marlborough" had arrived. Remington made a very impressive appearance in a dress suit, and word swiftly spread among the hotel help that "the Duke" was there in person. As a result he received a duke's attention. He thoroughly enjoyed the situation and made the most of it throughout the evening.

In 1889 the Remingtons moved from the small apartment on 58th Street to a more spacious home in a two-family house at 561 Mott Avenue in upper New York City. Next door to them was E. W. Kemble, whose friendship with Remington had begun in their Art Students League days, now also rising to a position as one of the country's important illustrators. It was this same year in which the Paris (France) Exposition awarded Remington the Silver Medal for his work; and the National Academy in its Autumn Exposition hung his large painting "A Dash For Timber" —a canvas that was destined to appear, on May 4, 1945, for sale at auction at the Kende Galleries in New York City, when the highest bidder was David Findlay, grandson of William W. Findlay, the Kansas City art dealer who had had the foresight to purchase Remington pictures long before his name meant anything at all in the field of art. "A Dash For Timber" brought $23,000—the largest sum ever paid for a Remington painting. Shortly afterward it was sold for a substantial profit to a private collector who presented it to the Fort Worth Club, Fort Worth, Texas, where it now hangs in a setting specially built for its display.

Even in 1889 Remington worked with almost equal facility in oil, water color, wash or pen-and-ink. According to his own admission pen-and-ink was "not natural" to him, although many of his early pictures were made in this medium. "I worked with it in the early days only to get away from the infernal wood engravers," he said. "Do not misunderstand me. I have no quarrel with the good engravers of the block— the men who are as much artists as those whose drawings they interpret . . . but my stuff was utterly strange to most people when I began picturing Western scenes."

It must be remembered that this was in the days when most magazine illustrations were reproduced from wood blocks carved by hand, and generally by other than the artist who created the original picture. To accomplish this the original was copied on a suitable-sized block of highly polished boxwood, lightly painted with a coating of china white so that it would take pencil, pen or brush. Sometimes the picture was copied freehand, although if the original had been made to the proper size a tracing was usually made and then rubbed down on the block. Naturally the copy on the wood block must be made entirely in reverse, so that it would appear correctly when the wood block was used for printing. To add to the hazard of true fidelity in the final result, these blocks were made in sections held together by steel bolts and separated so that, to save time, more than one woodcarver or "engraver" might work

58

FREDERIC REMINGTON

A FANTASY FROM THE PONY WAR DANCE
Harper's Monthly, December 1891

on it at the same time, after the picture had been transferred to its smooth surface. The block for a double-page spread for *Harper's Weekly* was usually made up of thirty-six pieces, and as many as four or more men would work independently at carving the sections which, when finally assembled again, printed a single picture. In the case of a line engraving, made from a pen-and-ink drawing, the original was far easier to copy upon the block and the carving did not involve the difficult shading required for a water color or oil painting. This explains why Remington used pen-and-ink, although he seems to have preferred to work in other mediums.

While most artists' work was copied on the wood block by other artisans, many of whom were very skilled and often appended their own names to the pictures they copied, this must not be confused with the double by-line beneath occasionally published pictures such as the first two Remingtons which appeared in *Harper's Weekly* in February 1882 and March 1885. These were cases in which the original pictures lacked the artistic qualities necessary for editorial approval, but had some particular merit which warranted giving them to a staff artist for re-drawing. Not long before, *Harper's Weekly* had published a picture of Colonial life under which was printed "Drawn by E. A. Abbey from a Sketch by Howard Pyle." That was before Pyle's wings were strong enough to enable him to fly alone. But Remington, like Pyle, once he got his stride, made a fast and furious race of it.

Beginning with his trip to the Southwest in the summer of 1888, Remington made a practice of going West at least once each year, even if he had a heavy schedule of work on hand. Usually, in addition to his main objective—to absorb the life of the West's fading frontier in order to perpetuate it in his work—he was on a specific assignment. In 1889, for instance, he traveled through Mexico to make sketches for the illustrations of Thomas A. Janvier's *The Aztec Treasure House* which began running in *Harper's Weekly* in December of that year. On this and several later trips he came to know the country below the Rio Grande as intimately as he knew the land north of the Border. The magnificence of the landscape and the picturesque, colorful people held an endless appeal for him, but even more perhaps he delighted in the fine Mexican horses.

Though he had sound enough practical reasons for these three-month excursions, it is probable that no lack of a sensible motive would have kept him home. It was Fred Remington's singular good fortune that the way of life he loved best should prove the very means by which he could best make his livelihood.

John Howard, from Ogdensburg, went with Remington on a trip to Mexico. During the journey they were entertained by a wealthy gentleman in Mexico City who had collected a large number of paintings by early Spanish and Italian masters. Mr. Howard was fond of telling how Fred trailed wearily along on the tour of the collection, wisely making no comments on a type of art with which he was unfamiliar and

60

unsympathetic, until, when it was apparent he could maintain his silence no longer, he forestalled questions as to his opinion of the paintings by asking in a sinking voice for a glass of water. Howard would add with a chuckle, "And God knows, a glass of water was generally the last thing in the world Fred Remington had any interest in!"

With other friends he went on expeditions to the Pacific Coast of Canada, fishing in the lakes of British Columbia, poking around mining camps in the Canadian Rockies, moose hunting, and fishing through the ice in Ontario.

A few statistics will perhaps most clearly indicate how diligently Remington was working and how far he had come in the four years between 1886 and 1890. During the latter year he had 119 illustrations in *Harper's Weekly* alone—including seven that were given double-page spreads—an average of over two for each week during the year. In the same year *Harper's Monthly* used thirty-six and *Century Magazine* eighteen Remington illustrations, with a few odds and ends thrown in elsewhere for good measure.

His most important order during 1890, and in some ways one of the most important he ever had, was to do twenty-two full-page plates and nearly four hundred text drawings for the Illustrated Edition of Henry Wadsworth Longfellow's poem *The Song of Hiawatha*.

The drawings for *Hiawatha* established Remington's reputation beyond venture of a doubt. The Illustrated Edition was enormously popular and it is not unlikely that the Remington illustrations did much to give the poem its cherished place in American literature. Many persons, even today, regard Remington's full-page pictures in this book as among the most inspired of his entire career. They had the further advantage of being reproduced in photogravure, rather than by the crude method of the wood block which was just then passing into obsolescence. Because of these pictures alone, Remington's name, when he was barely thirty years old and with such a comparatively short experience behind him, was already on the way to becoming a household word. If he had accomplished nothing more, it would entitle him to lasting renown. To appreciate just how far this artist had progressed in those brief four years, one need only compare some of the plates in *Hiawatha* with the best of his pictures that appeared in 1886 and '87. The same unmistakable Remington style characterizes them all, but the improvement is unmistakable.

CHAPTER IX

Studio to Sioux Warpath

DURING the late summer and fall of 1890 there were ominous threats of serious trouble in the Dakotas, where the rebellious Sioux under the fanatical guidance of Sitting Bull were believed to be planning a last mighty uprising. In an official report, General Miles stated: "The seriousness of the situation has not been exaggerated. . . . There are about 30,000 Indians affected . . . fully 6,000 of whom are fighting men . . . and 4,000 Indians can make an immense amount of trouble. . . . Every Indian 'buck' has a Winchester and he knows how to use it." Colonel Buffalo Bill Cody had been sent to arrest Sitting Bull, but had failed in the attempt. Additional troops were being rushed to the Pine Ridge Agency from other sections of the country.

All this portended the sort of thing which interested Remington most. Here was his old West about to break loose in its wildest aspect. So as winter began to settle in and it appeared more and more certain the climax was about to materialize, he headed west for the center of the trouble.

In early December troublesome old Sitting Bull and a host of his braves were participating in war dances in a large camp on the edge of the Bad Lands in South Dakota. He had gathered around him about four thousand of the fiercest and most daring renegades of the big Sioux tribe. He had convinced them that his powers as a medicine chief would protect them from the bullets of the white men, and that they could drive the intruders out of their country. Some Indians had already gone on the warpath. Five hundred head of government cattle and three hundred head belonging to Governor Millette of South Dakota had been slaughtered by the redskins and the beef hauled away in stolen wagons and pack trains to a stronghold in the Bad Lands.

General Miles was ready for any emergency, although his orders from Washington explicitly instructed him only to "arrest" Sitting Bull and to avoid a battle at all costs. A detail was sent to arrest the Sioux leader, the Indians started a fight, and Sitting Bull

62

with several of his subordinates was killed on December 15, 1890. The rest fled into the Bad Lands, with several groups of scouts and troops following in an effort to keep an eye on them, as best they could, and be on hand to act as a protection if the Indians decided to raid and massacre the residents of any of the posts or towns in the surrounding country.

It was in the midst of this excitement that Frederic Remington joined one of the scouting parties that was going into the Bad Lands. This was by no means a pleasure jaunt. It was serious Indian warfare and the first camp he made with the soldiers was on Christmas night, with the thermometer registering well below zero.

Through the instrumentality of General Miles, Remington was assigned to the scouting party led by Lieutenant E. W. Casey, one of the most accomplished officers in the Indian Scout service. He had in his command a particularly fine group of Cheyennes, with long and creditable records as aids to the United States Army, among whom were some of Remington's old acquaintances.

"Expansive smiles lit up the brown features of the Indian scouts as they recognized me," he recounted.* "Old Wolf-Voice came around in his large, patronizing way and said: 'How?—what you do here?' Wolf-Voice was a magnificent type of Indian, with a grand face, a tremendous physique, and enough self-containment for a High-Church bishop. High-Walking nudged Stump-Horn and whispered in his ear, and they both smiled as they looked at me. Lieutenant Casey walked out in the road and talked with General Miles, who sat on a beautiful sorrel horse, while two scouts and a young 'horse-pusher' from St. Louis helped me load one strawberry-roan horse into a box-car with a scrawny lot of ponies who showed the hard scouting of the last month."

After a short trip on the railroad, the scouting party was unloaded and struck out to make contact with the Sioux. A forced march brought them to the Cheyenne River, beyond which rose the tangled masses of the Bad Lands—"a place for stratagem and murder, with nothing to witness its mysteries but the cold blue winter sky . . . and it was full of savage Sioux."

A day's journey down the river brought them to the camp of another Army scouting party composed mostly of Indians from Pine Ridge. Two nights before, the Sioux had fired into the camp and there had been a skirmish. "The vermillion of the warpath was on every countenance, and, through sympathy, I saw that our men too had gone into this style of decorative art. . . .

" 'We go on the stronghold in the morning,' said Casey." The sun was not yet up when Remington swung onto his strawberry-roan to file away with Wolf-Voice and five other Cheyenne scouts. A mile below camp they undertook to cross the Cheyenne River.

* "The Sioux Outbreak in South Dakota," *Harper's Weekly*, Jan. 24, 1891.

"My horse was smooth shod, and the river frozen half-way over; so we slid around on the ice, and jumped into the icy water, got wet, crawled out, slid around some more and finally landed. Wolf-Voice looked me over and smilingly said: 'Me think you no like 'em'—wherein his conclusion was eminently correct. Who does like to have a mass of ice freeze on him when naturally the weather is cold enough to satisfy a walrus?'" But this was only the beginning.

Twelve miles through the defiles of the Bad Lands they trekked to the blue ridge of the high mesa where the hostile Indians had their main camp. The trail was strewn with dead cattle, some of them never having been touched with a knife. Here and there lay a dead pony, ridden to a standstill and left on the trail.

Shots are heard. They all stop to listen. Then they get out their guns and go galloping ahead like mad.

"I can't imagine why, but I spur my horse and perform equestrian feats which in an ordinary frame of mind I should regard as insane. Down a narrow trail we go, with the gravel flying, and through a *coulee*, up a little hill, on top of which we stop to listen; and then away we go again. The blue wall grows nearer, and at last we are under it. A few cottonwood trees, some frozen water, a little cleft on the bluffs, and I see a trail winding upward. I know these warriors are going up there, but I can't understand precisely how. It is not the first perilous trail I have contemplated; but there are dead cattle lying at the bottom, which had fallen off and been killed in the ascent.

"We dismount and start up. It tells on your wind and tries the leg muscles. Up a steep place a horse wants to go fast and you have to keep him from running over you. A bend in the trail where the running water has frozen seems impassable. I jump across it and then pull the bridle and say: 'Come on, Boy!' If I were the horse I would balk, but the noble animal will try it. A leap, a plunging and with a terrible scramble we are all right. Farther up, and the incline is certainly eighty-five degrees. My horse loses his front feet, but a jerk at the headstall brings him down and he plunges past me to be caught by an Indian at the top of the trail. For a moment we breathe, and then mount.

"Before us is a great flat plain blackened by fire with the grass still burning. Away in the distance, in the shimmer of the air waves, are figures.

" 'Maybe so dey Sioux,' says Wolf-Voice. And we gallop toward them.

" 'What will we do if they are?' I ask.

" 'Stand 'em off,' replies the war-dog.

"Half an hour's ride showed them to be some of our Cheyennes. All about the plain were strewn the remains of more dead cattle (heads and horns, half-butchered carcasses, and withal a rather impressive smell), coyotes and ravens—all very like war. There were lodge poles, old fires and a series of rifle pits across the neck of land which

64

the Sioux had prepared to defend; medicine poles and then the sacrifices, among which was food dedicated to the Great Spirit, but eventually consumed by the less exalted members of Casey's command. The Sioux had abandoned their stronghold. I vandalized a stone pipe and a rawhide stirrup.

"The less curious members of our band had gone south and Wolf-Voice and I rode along together."

Reaching the southern edge of the high mesa the pursuers could see the retreating hostile column and their rear scouts out on the great flats below. Casey's command gradually gathered at the edge of the bluff. A courier started his lonely ride back with a note for General Miles.

Presently a fast-riding horseman comes in to report. The Sioux have fired on the Army scouts. The order is given to move on. Guns are unslung and the air is full of fight. Night is approaching. Remington rides beside Lieutenant Casey and has a premonition of dire events ahead.

Lieutenant Casey's orders were to follow these wild-eyed Sioux and see that they did not commit massacre—*but to avoid warfare.* This was far from the idea of his Indian scouts. Even his old-time white scouts didn't like it.

" 'This is a new kind of war,' " grumbled an old soldier to Remington as they rode along. " 'Them Injuns don't understand it; and to tell you the truth, I don't neither. The Injuns say they have come all the way from Tongue River and are going back poor. Can't get Sioux horses; can't kill Sioux.' Then, shaking his shaggy head and tightening the wrinkles on his leathery face, he repeated: 'This is a new kind of war . . .' " and relapsed into reveries of things as they used to be before General Miles and the brass hats in Washington got queer notions.

As they shortened the distance to the Sioux, some of the Cheyennes and even the old soldiers broke ranks and showed signs of following their own more ancient theories. Lieutenant Casey, who was riding out ahead, wheeled his horse abruptly and with his hand on his six-shooter galloped back. With a look on his face that meant business, he snapped: " 'I'll shoot the first man through the head who falls out of ranks!' "

At the base of the bluff the column was halted and Casey rode on ahead alone for a powwow with a group of the Sioux who had stopped on a hill. Remington watched them through his field glasses and the rest stood nervously about waiting for something to happen.

At last Casey came back. He said nothing about the powwow, but it was plain he was not pleased. He ordered saddles off and told off heavy pickets for the night camp.

Darkness fell quickly and no one seemed to have much appetite for the meagre mess that each man prepared for himself.

Three or four Brulé Sioux were let in through the picket lines for a parley.

"I sat near the fire and looked intently at one human brute opposite. He was a perfect animal, so far as I could see. Never was there a face so replete with human depravity, stolid, ferocious, arrogant, and all the rest . . . ghost-shirt, war-paint, feathers and armed to the teeth. As a picture, perfect; as a reality, horrible."

They protested their good intentions; borrowed tobacco; told Lieutenant Casey he could send a wagon for commissaries to Pine Ridge; and that Remington could go through their lines with it.

The night was one of restlessness and apprehension. It was known that the Sioux were now on all sides of them, like wolves lurking in the darkness trying to find courage to attack.

The rest is best told by Remington himself:

"The next morning I announced my intention of going to Pine Ridge Agency, which is twenty-five miles away. Mr. Thompson, two scouts and a Swedish teamster are to go in for provisions and messages. Mr. Thompson ordered all guns put into the wagon and got in himself.

" 'If I can't talk them Injuns out of killing me,' he said, 'I reckon I'll have to go.'

"I trotted along with Red-Bear and Hairy-Arm, and a mile and a half ahead went the courier, Wells. Poor man! In two hours he lay bleeding in the road, with a bullet through the hips, and called two days for water before he 'struck the long trail to the kingdom-come.'

"After we had gone eight or ten miles and were just crossing a ravine we saw a Sioux buck on a little hill just ahead, out of pistol shot. Red-Bear turned his horse in the 'peace sign' and advanced. We drove over the ravine and halted. I dismounted. Six young Brulé Sioux rose from the ground and rode up to Red-Bear, and the hills became full of pickets to the right and left. We waited to hear the result of Red-Bear's conversation. When he came back he spoke to Thompson in Cheyenne. I looked at him and knew that the situation was bad.

" 'Red-Bear says we will have to go back,' explained Thompson, and turning to Red-Bear he requested that two Sioux might come closer and talk with us.

" 'This is a bad hole and I reckon our cake is dough right here,' said Thompson.

"Two young bucks came up and one asked Thompson for tobacco and he was handed a package of Durham, which was not returned. Another little buck slipped up behind me, whereat Mr. Thompson gave me a warning look. Turning, I advanced on him quickly (I wanted to be as near as possible, not being armed) and, holding out my hand, I said: 'How, colah?' He didn't like to take it, but he did, and I was saved the trouble of further action.

" 'We'll never get this wagon turned around,' suggested Mr. Thompson, as the teamster whipped up; but we did. And as we commenced our movement on Casey's camp, Mr. Thompson said: 'Go slow now; don't run, or they'll sure shoot.'

66

" 'Gemme gun,' said the little scout Red-Bear, and we all got our arms from the wagon.

"There was no suspense now. Things had begun to happen. A little faster, yet faster, we go up the little banks of the *coulee*, and, ye gods! what!—five fully-armed, well-mounted cowboys—a regular rescue scene from Buffalo Bill's show.

" 'Go back!' shouted Thompson.

"Bang! bang! bang! and the bullets whistle around and kick up the dust. Away we go.

"Four bucks start over the hills to our right to flank us. Red-Bear talked loudly in Cheyenne.

"Thompson repeated: 'If any one is hit, get off in the grass and lie down. We must all hang together.' 'We will!' we all yelled.

"The cowboys, being well mounted, could easily have gotten away, but they stuck like true blues. We deployed on the flanks of the wagon, so that the team horses might not be shot, which would have stopped the whole outfit, and we did ten miles at a record-breaking gallop. We struck the scout camp in a blaze of excitement. The Cheyennes were in war-paint and the ponies' tails were tied up and full of feathers. Had the Sioux materialized at that time, Mr. Casey would have had his orders broken right there.

"After a lull in the proceeding, Mr. Thompson confided to me that 'the next time I go to war in a wagon it will put the drinks on me'; and he saddled Piegan and patted his neck in a way which showed his gratification at the change in transport.

"We pulled out again for the lower country and as our scouts had seen the dust of Colonel Sanford's command, we presently joined them.

"How we awoke the next morning with the sleet freezing in our faces, and how we made camp in the blizzard, and borrowed Sibley stoves of the soldiers, and how we were at last comfortable, and spent New Year's Eve in a proper manner, is of little interest.

"I was awakened at a late hour that night by Captain Baldwin, of General Miles's staff, and told to saddle up for a night's ride to Pine Ridge. This was the end of my experience with Lieutenant Casey and his gallant corps. We shook hands cheerily in the dim candle-light of the tepee, and, agreeing to meet in New York at some not distant day, I stepped out of the Sibley, mounted and rode away in the night."

Just two days before Remington arrived at Pine Ridge Agency on December twenty-ninth, one of the other scouting parties located a camp on Wounded Knee Creek where about one third of Sitting Bull's followers were gathered under Chief Big Foot. This was not a great distance from the Pine Ridge Agency, and General Miles ordered Colonel Forsyth, of the Seventh U. S. Cavalry (General Custer's old regiment), to surround the renegade camp, disarm and arrest the Indians, and bring the leaders before him.

The weather was bitter cold—twenty degrees below zero. The camp was successfully surrounded; and the order was given for every brave to give up his rifle. At first they refused to obey. Then some produced their guns. An order to search the lodges was given. A rifle cracked from inside one of the lodges . . . the Indians began a mad scramble to get their weapons . . . more shots were fired . . . and the men of the Seventh opened fire without waiting for orders. Custer was avenged! But at cost of a good many brave members of his new Seventh Cavalry.

The now famous Wounded Knee Massacre was the last real battle between the Indians and the whites. It occurred on the same day that Remington left Lieutenant Casey's near-by camp and started on the two-day trip to Pine Ridge. They were bringing in the wounded when he reached the Agency.

Three days later, as Remington sat down in the dining car on the train that was taking him back to New York, he picked up a Chicago morning newspaper. The first thing he saw was the bold-type heading of one of the front-page columns: "Lieutenant E. W. Casey Shot."

It was an official dispatch from headquarters, reporting that Lieutenant Casey had been shot by Plenty Horses, one of the Brulé Sioux members of the same renegade band from which Remington had narrowly escaped only a few days before.

CHAPTER X

Indifference Abroad

THE Sioux uprising in the Bad Lands proved to be the last important episode in the long and dramatic chronicle of our Indian wars. It completed the conquest of the red man's domain, it marked the end of the Old West. There was a certain poetic justice in Frederic Remington's presence on the scene and, more practically, from this experience he drew a great number of articles, drawings and paintings, for his material was in the nature of a journalistic scoop. His articles, illustrated by himself, began appearing in *Harper's Weekly* with "The Sioux Outbreak in South Dakota" in the issue of January 24, 1891, followed by "Lieutenant Casey's Last Scout," January 31, and "The Sioux War," on February 7. Out of the sketches he had made on the spot developed some of his most dramatic paintings.

By 1892 he had bought a place in New Rochelle, not far north of New York City in Westchester County, which was something of an estate. The house itself was a large building in the pseudo-Gothic style so popular during the second half of the nineteenth century, with a tall, sharply gabled roof, a spacious front porch and wide stone steps. A broad lawn spread to the street three hundred feet away, and in the rear was a large stable where the master of the house kept the horses that were the pride of his possessions. The location, on the crest of a hill, gave a pleasant view overlooking the town, with a glimpse of Long Island Sound in the distance. It was an ideal place for a family of children, but the Remingtons, to their sorrow, remained childless.

Upstairs was a big workroom, under the high-gabled roof, where were stored a large assortment of saddles, harness, Indian and cowboy clothes, and even a life-sized dummy horse sometimes used to pose a human model.

His main studio was a large wing on the main floor, which he built onto the house shortly after occupying the place. It was twenty by forty feet on the floor, and twenty feet to the rooftree. Here at last was the studio of his dreams. A big skylight was set

69

in one pitch of the roof, and there were large windows across one end and side wall. The rear wall had a double door large enough to admit a pair of horses, or to be opened wide as he painted his live horse-models on the grounds outside. This famous studio was a place never to be forgotten by anyone who ever enjoyed the privilege of visiting it. There was a great fireplace, over which hung a monster moose head. The whole room was a veritable museum of things reminiscent of their owner's days in the West. Every available space of the four walls was covered with paraphernalia and artifacts of Indian and Mexican villages, trophies from lodge and warpath and all manner of gear of cowboys and military men. There were guns of practically every kind carried by an American pioneer or soldier; spurs and war bonnets; swords, bridles, saddles, powder-horns and knives; there were war clubs, tomahawks, bows, blood-stained arrows, tom-toms, peace pipes, human scalps and paraphernalia of medicine men; moccasins, beaded buckskin clothing; chalk-white buffalo skulls and a host of other fascinating mementoes of the wild frontier. Here also was always a fascinating array of his pictures, in various stages of completion—for it was here that he created his dashing and realistic portrayals of Western life. Here passed that constant parade of savage, half-civilized and glamorous actors, who came as the ghost-spirits of a thousand and one episodes of our Old West, to be re-born from the color-dipped tips of Remington's paint brushes and take form on his canvases.

On his many trips, the artist not only made a great many sketches of what he saw— many of his pictures are accurate portrayals of actual incidents he witnessed, even to the particular individuals involved—but he was also an eager and enthusiastic collector of all sorts of paraphernalia and decorations of Indians and frontiersmen.

But Remington was not a collector for pleasure only. Wherever possible he preferred not to rely on his memory or on hasty field sketches but to check details against an actual object and there was hardly an item in the vast array which was not used at one time or another to achieve the meticulous exactitude in particulars which helped to make his canvases an authentic record. He would go to any amount of trouble to acquire something he thought he might need in the future, though the pains he took were not always appreciated by his contemporaries. He enjoyed telling the story of a pair of fine Indian moccasins which he obtained on one of his early Western trips when he was with a small party of soldiers who, with a friendly Indian guide, were sent out to bring in a band of renegade Indians who had left the reservation without permission and showed signs of getting into serious trouble.

While cautiously approaching the renegades' camp the soldiers' presence was discovered and a volley of rifle shots caused the deploying party to drop to the ground behind whatever shelter was available. Remington found himself lying directly behind the Indian guide, who started firing his own rifle at the renegades who persisted in continuing potshots at the soldiers. For a time the artist's attention was solely oc-

TROOPER IN TOW
Century, April 1889

A HARD TRAIL
Century, March 1888

THE TEXAS TYPE OF COWBOY
Century, June 1888

APACHE SOLDIER OR SCOUT
Century, July 1889

cupied with watching nervously as the enemies' shots spattered in uncomfortable proximity. After a while, however, he noticed what a fascinating pair of beaded moccasins the Indian guide was wearing. They were almost in his face, and he examined them closely and admiringly.

"Want to sell those moccasins you have on?" questioned Remington.

The Indian carefully aimed his rifle, fired, and grunted: "Sell 'um . . . Dollar."

Remington squirmed until he could jam a hand in his pocket and extricate a dollar . . . but the guide was taking aim for another shot. After he had fired, Remington tossed him the dollar. The Indian kicked off the moccasins, pocketed the dollar . . . and returned to his rifle.

"I expected to get the moccasins after we returned to the reservation," explained Remington, "but it occurred to me that the guide or I might be killed, and in either case the bargain could not be concluded. So I closed the deal right on the spot and stuffed them into my pocket."

He laughed and added: "Later a model posing for me wore those particular moccasins, and when the picture was exhibited, an art critic wrote, 'Remington is always picturesque. His Indian guide wears a pair of moccasins the like of which were never worn by any Indian outside a theatre. The actual guide probably wore a pair of Army brogans!'"

A similar story related to a rifle in Remington's elaborate collection, which included nearly every model and pattern of gun ever used by United States soldiers since Colonial times. This particular rifle was also depicted in one of his pictures, which, when exhibited, brought forth a critic's condemnation that the gun was entirely out-of-place. The fact of the matter is that the rifle was one which had actually been used in the specific Indian campaign and the specific incident that was the subject of the picture. Criticism of that type from such sources did not bother him unduly. He continued to hew to his own line, and let the chips fall where they might.

As success in his chosen field became an accomplished fact, his always keen sense of independence and individuality rather increased than otherwise. The great masters of the past meant hardly more to him than Mozart or Beethoven would to chanting Sioux braves in a midnight scalp dance. He wanted no part of Europe, either its art or its languages, a fact which he made plain when Poultney Bigelow at the suggestion of *Harper's Monthly* proposed that they go abroad together. Remington "snorted with contempt," but Bigelow talked him into it. Probably no one else could have. In North Africa and the Sahara, Bigelow pointed out, Remington could see and sketch the blue-blooded ancestors of the plains' horses; he could visit the Kaiser's famous stud farm at Trakehnen, where the pride of the Prussian cavalry's mounts were bred and trained; see the spectacular riding of Russian Cossacks; and there would be, he promised, no visits to art museums.

They went first to the French colonies in North Africa, landing at Oran, Algeria, where they boarded a provincial train that was to take them to railhead at the edge of the Sahara Desert. The travelers settled themselves comfortably in the one first-class compartment and Remington, with a valise containing a prized bottle of Bourbon conveniently at hand, had just lit a large strong cigar when he suddenly leaped to his feet and bolted through the compartment door with an anguished cry, "Oh hell! Here comes a damned woman!" Brave though Remington was in facing wild horses and murderous men, he rigorously avoided the implications of casual chatter with women. And now he precipitated his portly proportions into the nearest second-class car amid the motley crowd of Kabyles, Moors and other nondescript travelers, rather than face the journey sharing the small compartment with a gracious French lady and her husband. It was with great difficulty, and some delay in starting the train, that Bigelow finally induced him to return.

Beyond the Atlas Mountains they were entertained with Arabian elegance by a desert chieftain, and here Remington was in his element. Here were the finest horses on earth and horsemen who could equal in riding skill anything even the Old West could offer. They were welcomed by the mad charge of a squadron of mounted Arabs, who sprang out of ambush and raced upon them with apparent fury and the firing of guns, throwing their cream-white horses back upon their haunches an instant before running them down. Remington was so busy sketching that he hardly took time to eat or renew acquaintance with the bottle of Bourbon in his valise.

From Africa they crossed the Mediterranean bound for Russia, where they planned to make a long journey by river in two specially built canoes that had been shipped from the United States. They arrived in St. Petersburg on June 6, 1892, and immediately presented their credentials to the authorities preparatory to receiving the proper permits for carrying out their plans. But after numerous postponements and rebuffs and endless trips to various offices, they decided that "the Russian government was very jealous of foreigners who came to report on things Russian,"* and finally were told "urbanely, that they had come on a fool's errand." They were furnished caviar, champagne and what appeared to be lordly hospitality, Russian style, but no permission was forthcoming to sail their specially built canoes upon any Russian water, or take notes, or make sketches. The letters they received while waiting were all opened, apparently by the police, and clumsily sealed again; and everywhere they went they were followed and closely watched. While driving one day in the suburbs, Remington noticed that he was being followed by an official in another droshky which soon passed him and stopped some way ahead while the official spoke to a gendarme. When Remington's vehicle reached the gendarme his horse was turned back toward the city after the driver had been given some special instructions which Remington naturally

* Poultney Bigelow, *Seventy Summers*.

couldn't understand, and it wasn't long before he was unwillingly deposited at his hotel venting his feelings in Western expletives at everything Russian.

After lengthy diplomatic efforts had failed to gain the necessary permits, they were "politely requested to disappear from Russia in the shortest possible time." Furious and baffled, they considered proceeding without permits or further formality, but were dissuaded by a friend who pointed out what the inevitable result would be. " 'You will be arrested at the first convenient place and kept a week or so pending examination . . . or some dark night you will have your canoes smashed to kindling, your stores, papers and valuables taken away and yourselves turned adrift in a swamp.'

" 'But,' protested Poultney Bigelow, 'you don't mean to say that a great government would permit such a thing?'

" 'Of course not! Our great government would express the most profound regret at the accident; it would insist that the damage was done not by police agents, but by common thieves.' "†

Remington and Bigelow got out of Russia.

Some days were spent inspecting the stock on Emperor William's stud farm and they saw the Kaiser's hunting lodge and royal hunting forest at Rominten. But Remington was ready for home, and less than three weeks after leaving St. Petersburg he had arrived in London, where he wrote to the traveling companion he had left behind in his hurry:

> MY DEAR BIGELOW, I have got some London clothes and am a very nice young man, but have great difficulty with the cab drivers whose pronunciation of English is so different from mine. . . .

By a happy coincidence, Buffalo Bill's Wild West Show was playing in London and naturally Remington lost no time in seeing it.

"One should no longer ride the deserts of Texas or the rugged uplands of Wyoming to see the Indians or the pioneers, but should go to London," he wrote.‡ "It is also quite unnecessary to brave the fleas and the police of the Czar to see the Cossack, or to tempt the waves which roll between New York and the far-off Argentine to study the 'Gauchos.' It is all in London.

"The gauchos are dressed in a sort of Spanish costume, with tremendous pantaloons of cotton and boots made of colt's skin, which in their construction are very like Apache moccasins. They carry a knife at their back which would make a hole a doctor couldn't sew up with less than five stitches, if indeed he was troubled at all. They ride a saddle which one of the American cowboys designated as a '——feather bed,' and they talk Spanish which would floor a Castilian at once. They ride bucking horses by pairs and amuse the audience by falling off at intervals.

† Poultney Bigelow, "Why We Left Russia," *Harper's Monthly*, Jan., 1893.
‡ "Buffalo Bill's Wild West Show in London," *Harper's Weekly*, Sept. 3, 1892.

"The great interest which attaches to the whole show is that it enables the audience to take sides on the question of which people ride best and have the best saddles."

That Fred Remington did not remain meekly seated on a bench while a part of his own world cavorted before him is indicated by his further comments regarding the trials and tribulations of the show's manager. It seems that the performers were split into bitterly jealous factions, that the American cowboys had to be penalized by deductions from their pay-checks to prevent them from standing on their heads on horseback in imitation of the Cossacks, that the Indians all ate too much, that impersonal arguments about the comparative merits of different types of saddles had a fatal tendency to develop into personal fisticuffs, and that each one of them was thoroughly schooled in the theory that it was only proper to run a ten-inch knife into the anatomy of anyone who did not agree with his particular way of thinking. With all of which Remington was completely and joyfully at home.

Whatever impression European art made upon him—and there is not the slightest evidence that it made any at all—he was definitely affected by the numbers of military men in uniform and the persistent display of their tools of warfare. It reminded him of a war dance in the Indian country, and it meant to him just one thing—war.

"I am afraid I shall never grow to like Europe," he wrote to Poultney Bigelow, after returning home. "The language is not as good as English and my bump of reverence is a hole. But the War! I'll do that—English or no English." And in another letter he said, "It looks to a man up a tree just as though there would be a scrap in the spring. I think the Russian border is our place—two horses apiece and an orderly, I suppose. Tell me how best I can go at this thing, since I'm going to see that war if I have to enlist."

Yet his personal philosophy gave him no love for the mechanized armies and impersonalized warfare clearly foreseeable even then. Before sailing for home he had a chance to see the Military Games at Aldershot, and his account of the spectacle is illuminating:§

"It is a great pity that the pitiless, all-penetrating, rapid-firing rifle cannot be traded for the 'gray goose's wing,' and all these miserable machinating staff and ordinance officers and inventors be relegated to the devil, when once again war and fighting should make men glad and death easy. Oh, sorry the day—of steamships and box-cars and Nordenfelts and British interests! If again could come the times when the 'tall fellows of England' could drop over the Channel and 'spit' a few French, or follow one lord to conclusions against his fellow lord!—when, as Philippe de Comines said, 'it presented the rare spectacle of a land when there are no buildings destroyed or demolished by war, and where the mischief of it falls on those who make war!' But we fear for the future; a few more 'boxes of tricks,' say balloons and dyna-

§ "The Military Athletics at Aldershot," *Harper's Weekly*, Sept. 10, 1892.

mite in conjunction, and it will become necessary to give over fighting altogether. What will take the place of fighting? Talk and subterfuge, more international law and men trained from boyhood to lie and dissemble. I suppose this will be it. Then cowards will be even more respected than they are now, and the fittest to survive will not be the ones with strong backs, the perfect nerve force and the red blood in their necks. The Orientals may come again in those days. If Mr. Edison and his fellows will only confine themselves to inventions of civil importance there is yet hope that the rapid-fire guns will get out of order, that the machinery in the big ships will not work properly in action, and that the balloon may be carried out of its course by the wind."

He never got over his aversion to things European. Five years later he wrote to Poultney Bigelow: "No, honey, I should not try Europe again. I am not built right —I hate parks—collars—cuffs—foreign languages—cut and dried stuff. Europe is all right for most everybody but me—I am going to do *America*—it's new—it's to my taste. . . . Have been catching trout and killing deer—feel bully—absolutely on the water wagon, but it don't agree with me. I am at 240 pounds and nothing can stop me but an incurable disease."

CHAPTER XI

A Man's Man

THE fact that Remington now had practically all the illustrating work he could handle, did not satisfy him—and he had little interest in anything but his beloved West. But the contribution which he was making to a lasting history of land beyond the Mississippi was gaining for him a steadily increasing recognition. On January 7, 1892, only six years after the first Remington picture appeared over his name in a magazine, the great historian Francis Parkman wrote him the following letter, which was prompted by his being selected by the publishers to draw the pictures for an illustrated edition of Parkman's famous classic *The Oregon Trail:*

> I am very glad that you are to illustrate the *Oregon Trail,* for I have long admired your rendering of Western Life, as superior to that of any other artist. You have seen so much and observed so closely that you have no rival in this department.
>
> F. PARKMAN.

In the Preface to that edition, under date of September 16, 1892, and published just before Parkman's death, the historian had this further to say:

> The Wild West is tamed and its savage charms have withered. If this book can help to keep their memory alive, it will have done its part. It has found a powerful helper in the pencil of Mr. Remington, whose pictures are as full of truth as of spirit, for they are the work of one who knew the prairies and the mountains before irresistible commonplace had subdued them.

The Oregon Trail, published in 1892, marked another important milestone in Frederic Remington's career.

On January 6, 1893, he held his first public exhibition, which may be considered his first serious step from the field of illustration into the sphere of professional artist. It is true that practically all of the one hundred drawings and paintings had been made for, and used as, illustrations; but the originals were now openly hung as an invitation to

77

the scrutinizing gaze of critics; and at the end of the one week exhibition all of the pictures were placed upon the auction block.

"An event of importance in any artist's career is his first exhibition and sale of pictures," wrote the editor of *Harper's Weekly* in the issue of January 1, 1893:

> The uncertainty as to the result is often stronger in his mind than in the minds of his friends, yet there is always the uncertainty, followed often by great success where little was looked for, and sometimes by little where much was deserved. Mr. Frederic Remington, who has exhibited so much of his best and always effective work in the pages of the *Weekly*, is about to undergo his first ordeal of this kind. One hundred of his pictures will be exhibited for one week from Friday, January 6, in the gallery of the American Art Association in Twenty-third Street, New York City. The collection will include some of Mr. Remington's largest and most ambitious canvases illustrating scenes accompanying the conquest of our West. There will be a great number of smaller American pictures in oil and water color and black and white. A few of the subjects are the result of the artist's recent trip to Germany and Russia. The host of admirers of Remington's work as an illustrator will be more than ever gratified by his skill as a painter.

Ninety-six of the pictures were sold, bringing a total of $7,005. This was an average of approximately $73 each, although the highest price was $410 and some of the small sketches went for as low as $13. On the whole, the exhibition and sale were not considered particularly successful.

Shortly afterward, he and John Howard, his old friend and companion on previous trips, went off again to the back country of Mexico where the six-gun was still the principal law of the land. Their destination was the hacienda San José de Bavicora, northwest of Chihuahua "two hundred and twenty-five of the longest miles on the map," as Remington expressed it. On the last part of the trip they bumped over stones and through blinding dust for five long days in the *patrón's* ranch coach—no one went to Bavicora unless specially invited.

San José de Bavicora was a little empire, far removed from the rest of the world, and ruled by one man. Thousands of head of cattle roamed its vast rugged ranges, herded by picturesque *vaqueros;* it took four days to ride around the outer boundary of the ranch, and within its confines was about as wild an outpost of civilization as it was possible to find in North America. Its history went back to 1770 when it had been built by the Jesuits. Apaches wiped out the community in 1840 and the place remained devastated and deserted, crumbling back into dust, until 1882 when an American cowboy wandering south from Arizona looked down across its wide fair plains from the mountains. Taking a fancy to the place he said, "I will take this," and with his two hardy cowpuncher companions, Jack Gilbert, or Don Gilberto as he became known, moved in and made good his decision.

The story of his long and strenuous struggle against the Apaches who, even in 1893, were still very much in evidence, and how as *patrón* Jack built the great

78

ROPED!
Century, April 1888

FIGHT IN THE STREET
Century, October 1888

PULLING A COW OUT OF THE MUD
Century, February 1888

hacienda of San José de Bavicora, is one of the most fascinating and unusual episodes in American pioneering. Remington told it, with the account of his own experiences there, in several illustrated articles in *Harper's Monthly:* "An Outpost of Civilization," December 1893; "In the Sierra Madre with the Punchers," February 1894; and "A Rodeo at Los Ojos," March 1894.

Though the Southwest had a peculiar charm for him, Remington liked everything associated with the out-of-doors. Once at least he went to the North Woods in midwinter on a spur-of-the-moment decision. When Julian Ralph complained at The Players that he was tired from overwork and had gone stale, Remington prescribed a trip to some wild frontier, insisting that it was the best of all possible remedies and deciding, on second thought, that it was exactly what his own condition required. The proper place to indulge in the treatment, he said, was in the snow-covered woods of Canada, and the sooner they got started the better.

"Within twenty-four hours we can be tracking moose near Hudson Bay," he argued.

Bright and early the next morning he and Ralph boarded the train for Montreal, not knowing what their ultimate destination would be. From Montreal they sent a number of telegrams to Hudson's Bay Company posts situated in likely moose-hunting districts, and they eventually found themselves trailing their game through the winter-bound forests north of Mattawa, Ontario. Julian Ralph embodied his account of the expedition, with others they made together, in his book *On Canada's Frontier.*

Remington's interests were extremely masculine. It has been stated by more than one commentator that he never drew or painted a picture of a woman—and this has become one of the popular and not entirely true beliefs about him. "His greatest admirer must search in vain through all the artist's pictures and bronzes for a petticoat," wrote Charles B. Davis.* "The pretty schoolmistress from the East, the rough woman of the mining camp with her heart of gold concealed by her brazen finery, the miner's daughter with her sombrero, the quick wit and unerring aim of her ever-ready six-shooter—all of which have proven such excellent material in the hands of Bret Harte and Owen Wister, and all other writers and artists of our Western life—have been wholly neglected by Remington." All of which is truly "in character" for Frederic Remington. If any of our artists deserve the distinction of being strictly a painter of men and a man's man, it certainly is Remington. It is true that few feminine characters ever got into the masculine sanctum of his work. The Indians and Mexicans he portrayed, the observer might easily conclude had neither mothers, mates, nor sweethearts. But his masculinity was not carried to the extent of total exclusion. In his own book *John Ermine of the Yellowstone*—his one attempt at a novel with a love motive —he employed another, Charles Dana Gibson, to draw the pictures of his leading feminine character. Only one of the feminine pictures in that book ("He Bore the

---

* "Remington—The Man and His Work," *Collier's,* Mar. 18, 1905.

Limp Form to the Sands"—page 209) was drawn by the author. But there are other women among Remington's illustrations. For example, those in Julian Ralph's article "Where Times Have Slumbered," in *Harper's Monthly*, September 1894; for Poultney Bigelow's accounts of the trip on which Remington accompanied him to Europe; "The Military Search For Belle McKeever," in *Harper's Weekly*, December 16, 1899; and a number of others. He even drew a nude woman—which appeared as a half-page reproduction in Mr. Hearst's New York *Journal* on February 12, 1897. This bore the caption "Spaniards Search Women on American Steamer" as an illustration accompanying a bitterly anti-Spanish article by Richard Harding Davis on the situation in Cuba, and both article and picture stirred American public sentiment to such an extent that some commentators claim they contributed toward the Spanish-American War. While Remington did include pictures of women in his repertoire, it must be emphasized that they are comparatively few and the artist strongly preferred to devote his time to masculine subjects.

This aversion to portraying the female was something he seems to have inherited along with his liking for horses, rugged individualism and unadulterated Americanism. There are no pictures of girls in his boyhood sketch books. When first beginning to apply himself with seriousness to drawing, while still a young man in Kansas City, he was asked to make a sketch of the baby of a friend for whom he held a deep esteem; but he refused on the grounds that the result was sure to make the child look like a papoose. Instead, he drew a portrait of the family horse. He also admitted laughingly that he almost lost Missie, very shortly after their marriage, when he had her pose for one of his early pictures. "She looked like a Mexican woman of the most ordinary desert type!" he admitted later. It is also significant that he never applied his efforts to the Western dance hall and its painted females—to some so appealing a phase of the Western scene.

With all women, except his own family and a few intimate friends, he was shy and sometimes inclined to gruffness. Eva enjoyed polite social occasions, and Frederic, who was a devoted husband, could occasionally be prevailed upon to accompany her. They attended the informal dances held at David's Island (now Fort Slocum), an artillery post at which several batteries were stationed. Mrs. Martha Summerhayes gave an account of a meeting with Remington there. She was the wife of Major Jack Summerhayes, a friend and hunting companion, so that she did not paralyze him as utterly as a stranger might have, yet he could find no small talk with which to entertain her. She complimented him on his work, for it appealed to Army people, and he seemed pleased but relapsed almost immediately into glum silence, his eyes fixed on a flag stretching across the end of the hall from behind which some soldiers, who were going to assist in serving the supper, were passing in and out. Mrs. Summerhayes asked him what he was looking at and he replied that he wished he were back there with the soldiers. "Those are the men I like to study," he stammered. "I don't like this fuss and feather of society." Then he blushed in realization of his lack of gallantry, asked her to dance, seized her and whirled her around at an incredible pace, and deposited her at the end of a turn with a gasp of relief and the remark, "That's enough of this sort of thing, isn't it?"

Eva Remington was gentle, understanding and loving, in a rôle not without its shadows. Under her tender but powerful influence, he made great efforts to overcome his weakness for drinking and was constantly "going on the wagon." "The latest news is," he wrote to Poultney Bigelow on May 15, 1894, "that I haven't had a drink in three weeks, and ain't going to have any more till I am about to die, when, after consultation of physicians, I am going to take one martini before I go up the Golden Stairs. I feel better. Have been up North for two weeks in training. Did fifteen miles a day on foot and am down to 210 pounds. . . . I have been sick for two years and didn't know it. Too much rum." And a year later, again to Bigelow: "I have concluded, or did conclude sometime ago, to quit drinking. I reasoned that I had had all of that kind of fun that one man could expect to have and do anything else; so I cut square off and feel better. But I am not a damned bit sorry about any drink I ever had. I only hope to die sane enough to feel that whatever I do is right—since I *mean* to do right."

He was a man of great gusto and energy and love of the good things in life, with an immense capacity for hard work. He held to the routine of his days of struggle; up very early, breakfast at seven (pigs' knuckles, if he had his choice), then to work until three o'clock. Whistling, singing, smoking, occasionally taking a nip from a bottle beside his easel, he worked whether he felt in the mood for it or not. For all the vast quantity he turned out, he continued to be a stickler for detail; he once toiled for days to achieve the effect of raindrops bouncing on the calm surface of water, and to get exactly right such small details as the single line defining the leg of a horse galloping in the distance was always important to him.

The rest of the day was generally devoted to relaxation. He never gave up tennis or ping-pong, though he finally was forced to invent a stick with a suction cup on the end for picking up the balls without bending over. But it was a sad day indeed when he grew so heavy that bicycling and walking became the inevitable substitutes for riding and jumping fences on his thoroughbred Irish hunter.

Remington's home life was paradoxical in view of his whole field of art and expression in which everything was so raw and rugged. Home to most of his characters was little more than sweaty, smelly saddle blankets laid on the hard earth beneath stars with the cold stare of steel. But to Frederic Remington, his wife and his home were sacred. His devotion to both was deep and sincere. His favorite evening was that one spent alone with Missie, or "Kid" as he called her in later years, in the big studio with its easy chairs, spreading fireplace and wealth of Western atmosphere.

CHAPTER XII

"He Knew the Horse"

IN ADDITION to his aversion to portraying anything which had the semblance of femininity, there are two other important characteristics in his work which had roots deep in Frederic Remington's personality. One was a theme of tense struggle against almost overwhelming odds; and the other was the predominance of horses in his pictures and his inspired genius as their delineator.

Remington's struggle motif is evident in such pictures as "The Last Lull in the Fight," "Fight for the Water Hole" and other such pictures in which small groups of frontiersmen or soldiers are fighting to the death against an overwhelming fate which seems slowly closing in upon them. At other times it takes the form of man or beast pitted desperately against the blistering desert, freezing winter or some other form of nature in her cruelest mood.

From his earliest boyhood sketch books to the last canvases on which he spread his paints, Western horses and the men who rode them are preponderant. The fact that his father distinguished himself as a cavalry officer undoubtedly had something to do with the beginning of this interest. As C. M. Fairbanks wrote about him in 1896: "It brought this promising infant into horsey surroundings almost at birth. That noble animal, now being nearly displaced in our domestic economy by the bicycle, was the earliest plaything and companion of the horse's ablest delineator of the future."*

Very early in life he became an exceptionally good rider. This ability, probably more than his sturdy physique and compatible temperament, gained for him the comradeship of the cowboys and Indians of the West, among whom he found the material for his career. The horse was always his principal interest, outside of his wife and his work—and it was one of the mainstays of his work.

Frederic Remington was by no means the first artist who loved to portray horses. There had been many before him, dating back through many centuries. Nor was he

* "Artist Remington at Home and Afield," *Metropolitan Magazine,* July 1896.

the first to portray a horse racing with all four feet off the ground—a credit which has often disputably been attributed to him. But the claim that he gave more real animated fire and life to the horses he portrayed than any other artist who preceded him, is a tribute no one could deny him. The manner in which he pictured this noble animal was, at the time, considered the most unconventional aspect of his work. Previously, for centuries, most artists had given their equine subjects something of the stolid rigidity of children's hobbyhorses, on which their riders sat as stiffly as toy soldiers. Most of those who dared to portray a horse supposedly running at full speed or taking a jump, pictured it as skimming over the ground with all four legs spread out horizontally—like a frozen rabbit. But Remington's horses were different. His were the wild horses of the West, and they were, from the start, as lithe, flexible and alive in his pictures as in nature. He drew them standing almost erect on their hind legs, or on their front feet, or even doubled up with their legs jackknifed under their bellies "like crabs." And he made a bold habit of picturing them with all four feet off the ground. For this revolutionary boldness he was criticized and ridiculed, not only by critics of art but by authorities on horses. His vindication, however, was not long in coming; and it came in a manner which even the most incredulous could not dispute. Professor Muybridge's discoveries made through instantaneous photography demonstrated beyond all argument the fact that horses did at times travel with *all four feet off the ground*. But Remington's keen eye had already been his own instantaneous camera.

Of equal importance is the fact that every horse was, to Remington, different from every other horse, not only in its lines and color, but in disposition and characteristics. He added personality and character to the horses he portrayed.

The horses of our Western plains quite naturally interested him more than any others and he was a real authority on the subject. When he was still in his twenties, he wrote a comprehensive article on "The Horses of the Plains," which appeared in *Century Magazine*, January 1889.

He had carefully traced and studied the history of the Western bronco, following its ancestry and development back through the nearly four centuries since the original Spanish invaders of Mexico first brought horses to this continent. He knew the characteristics of the horses ridden by Francisco Coronado and his followers northward from Mexico, as far as what is now Kansas, three quarters of a century before the Pilgrims landed on Plymouth Rock; and he knew the sort of horses De Soto and his soldiers, even before Coronado, had ridden westward from Florida across the Mississippi.

The introduction of the horse to North America by the early Spanish explorers proved to be of tremendous benefit to the Indians, particularly to the plains Indians who were largely dependent for food upon the vast herds of buffalo and other big game, and who had previously been compelled to do all their hunting on foot. Rem-

84

BRINGING HOME THE GAME
Century, June 1888

PIKE COUNTY ARRIVALS
Century, December 1890

ington had gone deeply into why and how the various tribes had acquired and developed their own breeds. He found that the horse of northern Mexico was "in size, bone and general development . . . the best among his kind," because "the Mexicans on their Indian-infested frontier kept their horses closely herded; for they lived where they had located their ranches, desired good horses and took pains to produce them." He pointed out that "the good representatives of this division are about fourteen and a half hands in stature; of large bone, with a slight tendency to roughness; generally bay in color; flat-ribbed, and of great muscular development; and, like all the rest, have the Barbary head, with the slightly oval face and fine muzzle."

The "pinto" or "painted" ponies, prime favorites of the Comanches, Wichitas and Kiowas, and highly prized by prosperous chiefs and warriors of the more northern tribes, varied in some respects according to locality. Of those found in the sun-baked desert regions, Remington wrote:

"Any old cowboy will point him out as the only creature suitable for his purpose. Hard to break, because he has any amount of latent devil in his disposition. He does not break his legs or fall over backward in the 'pitching' process as does the 'cayuse' of the northwest. He is small and shriveled up like a Mexican, because of his dry, hot habitat, over which he has to walk many miles to get his dinner. Once in Arizona I rode one of these animals, belonging to Chief Ascension of the Papagoes, at a very rapid gallop for twenty-four miles, during the middle of the day, through the desert sand. The thermometer stood as high as you please in the shade, and the hot sun on the white sand made the heat something frightful; and personally I am not noted for any of the physical characteristics which distinguish a fairy. At the end of the journey I was confirmed in the suspicion that he was the most magnificent piece of horseflesh for a ride like that, and I never expect to see another horse which can make such a trip and take it so lightly to heart. He stood there like a rock, and was as good as at starting, having sweat only a normal amount. The best test of a horse is, not what he can do, but how easily he can do it."†

In tracing the history of the "Cherokee pony" of the Indian Territory, Arkansas and Missouri, Remington found that it derived from the East, rather than from the Western bronco as most observers believed.

From the haciendas of Old Mexico to the blizzard-swept winter prairies and forests of the Canadian Northwest and the Pacific slopes of the Rockies, Remington knew every variety of horse which had been developed in the Old West. To him, there was as much difference between a "mustang," "cayuse," "Oregon horse," and the several other breeds, as there was between the many Indian tribes which he knew with equal familiarity and discrimination.

Remington also made his contribution to the age-old controversy between advocates

† "The Horses of the Plains," *Century Magazine,* Jan., 1889.

of the Western saddle and those favoring the Eastern or European style of horsemanship. It is not surprising to find him on the side of the Westerners, though he gave the other a fair trial:

"I had occasion to ride a stock saddle, which is the cowboy article, and held all other trees and methods of riding in a magnificent contempt. Later on I had to be convinced that a great many young cavalry officers in our service were the most daring and perfect riders, and that the McClelland saddle was the proper thing. I even elaborated a theory in explanation of this, which I had duly shattered for me when I went East and frequented a New York riding academy, where a smiling professor of the art assured me that cowboys and soldiers were the worst possible riders. Indeed, the sneers of the polite European were so superlative that I dared not even doubt his statements. Of course I never quite understood how my old companions of the cattle range and the war trail could pick things off the ground while in full career, or ride like mad over the cut banks and boulders, if they were such desperately bad riders; and I never was able to completely understand why any European master could hardly turn in his saddle without tumbling off. But still he reduced me to submission and I ceased even to doubt.

"I changed my style of riding, in deference to a public sentiment, and got my legs tucked up under my chin and learned to loose my seat at every alternate footfall; and in time acquired a balance which was as secure as a pumpkin on the side of a barrel. Thus equipped with all this knowledge and my own saddle, I went out to the northwest with the purpose of introducing a little revolution in cavalry riding.

"Things went swimmingly for a time. The interpreters and scouts watched my riding with mingled pity and scorn, but I knew they were unenlightened and in no way to be regarded seriously. General Miles was duly amused by my teetering and suggested to the smiling escort officers that 'he lived so long abroad, you know,' etc.— all of which I did not mind, for my faith in the eternal art of the thing was complete. But I soon discovered that I was riding a seat which was no seat at all and was only retained by a series of happy accidents. . . .

"For a smooth road and a trotting horse, that European riding-master was right; but when you put a man in the dust or smoke, over the rocks and cut banks, on the 'bucking' horse, or where he must handle his weapons or his *riata*, he must have a seat on his mount as tight as a stamp on an envelope, and not go washing around like shot in a bottle. In a park or on a country road, where a man has nothing to do but give his undivided attention to sticking on his saddle, it has its advantages. But an Indian or a cowboy could take the average park rider off from his horse, scalp him, hang him on a bush and never break a gallop.

"In intelligence the bronco has no equal," he contended, "unless it is the mule, though this comparison is inapt, as that hybrid has an extra endowment of brain, as though in compensation for the beauty which he lacks. The wild state may have sharpened the senses of the bronco, while in domestication he is remarkably docile. Everyone knows that he 'bucks,' and familiarity with that characteristic never breeds contempt. Only those who have ridden a bronco the first time it was saddled, or has lived through a railroad accident, can form any conception of such an experience. His greatest quality is the ease with which he stands any amount of hard riding on the trail.

"As a saddle animal simply, the bronco has no superior. But this particular American horse lays claim to another quality, which in my estimation is not least, and that is his wonderful picturesqueness. He graces the Western landscape, not because he reminds us of the equine ideal, but because he comes of the soil, and has borne the heat and burden and the vicissitudes of all that pale of romance which will cling about the Western frontier. As we see him hitched to the plow or the wagon he seems a living protest against utilitarianism; but, unlike his red master, he will not go. He has borne the Moor, the Spanish conqueror, the red Indian, the mountain-man, and the *vaquero* through all the glories of their careers; but they will soon be gone, with all their heritage of gallant deeds. The pony must meekly enter the new regime. He must wear the collar of the new civilization and earn his oats by the sweat of his flank. There are no more worlds for him to conquer; now he must till the ground."‡

No better concluding emphasis can be given to Frederic Remington's deep and inherent interest in horses than the only personal eulogy that he was ever known to have desired. "When I die," he said on a number of occasions to intimate friends, "I would like to have my epitaph read: 'HE KNEW THE HORSE.'"

‡ Frederic Remington, "Chasing a Major-General," *Harper's Weekly*, Dec. 6, 1890.

CHAPTER XIII

From Paint to Bronze

B Y 1895 Frederic Remington was recognized as one of America's foremost magazine and book illustrators, and one of the world's foremost exponents in art of our wild Western scene. His pictures of horses in action were warmly admired wherever men knew horseflesh and his name had already taken on a synonymity with things Western. He had also been accepted as an important writer on the West. His first book, *Pony Tracks*, appeared at this time. It was a selection of fifteen of his best articles from *Harper's Weekly* and *Harper's Monthly* together with the best of the illustrations that had appeared with them, and today a copy in good condition is a collector's item of considerable value. To many readers, including the reviewer on the Boston *Transcript*, it gave "a better idea of army life on the Western border than all the official records that were ever written."

Whatever he had done, irrespective of the medium in which he chose to express himself, he had held steadfast to that thesis with which he had begun his career. The technique and conception of his work had continued to improve, although his distinctly individual style had remained the same.

As we look upon Frederic Remington's pictures and other work today, there are but very few among us who can evaluate them with the benefit of having personally seen and known the scenes and the times he portrayed. But when Remington was producing and offering his work for recognition, there were plenty who could criticize every detail with the trained eye and feeling of an expert. It is significant, and no small compliment, that those who had played their own part in the drama of the Old West and knew it best were among Remington's most ardent admirers.

Under date of November 20, 1895, on stationery of the Police Department of New York City, the following letter, which bears quoting, was written to Remington:

I never so wished to be a millionaire or indeed any other person than a literary man with a large family of small children and taste for practical politics and bear hunting, as when you have pictures to sell. It seems to me that you in your line, and Wister in his, are doing the best work in America today.

THEODORE ROOSEVELT.

In spite of success, his ambition to become a distinguished artist and paint important pictures in his chosen field, rather than an illustrator following other people's specifications, was still an unsatisfied desire. It must be remembered, however, that he was still a comparatively young man. October 1, 1895 was only his thirty-fourth birthday; and at that time he had less than ten years of professional experience behind him. He had climbed rapidly and turned out an unusual amount of work; but it had been a hard struggle, under the difficulties of a rather dogmatic determination to accomplish his objective without the benefits of outside assistance or influence, as well as the handicap of being compelled to make his work provide a livelihood at the same time. The summer of 1895, however, marked a very definite turning point toward the fulfillment of his great desire. Bolstered by the feeling of comparative security which his position as an accomplished illustrator gave him, and the realization that he had mastered his profession, he began to look seriously to more distinguished fields to conquer.

His first real step outside the field of illustration and into the realm of pure art was as sculptor. This broad chasm was bridged in a manner which is one of the high spots of Remington's career; and his masterly portrayal of the horse took on a new dimension both literally and figuratively.

In his drawing and painting, he visualized his figures on all sides—which gave him a natural aptitude for sculpturing. As an example of this, his friend Augustus Thomas tells of watching him at work on an illustration for one of Owen Wister's stories.* He was just beginning the picture; and he was working "chic," or without models. With sketchy lines in charcoal the outline began to take shape. It showed a Westerner in the foreground of a barroom, with his six-guns pointed toward a group of men in the picture's background. Suddenly, with a terse comment that the figure in the foreground obscured too much of the interesting detail in the background, Remington quickly wiped off the charcoal drawing and completely reversed the field of his characters. In a very short time he had sketched in his shooting Westerner in the background where he did not obstruct the rest of the scene. With the greatest of ease he could turn any of his pictured subjects about—front, side, or back, as the impulse prompted him. Whether it was Indian, white man or horse, he knew and saw them from every angle. Realizing this, Augustus Thomas said to him: "Fred, you're not a draftsman; you're a sculptor. You saw all around that fellow, and could have put him anywhere you wanted him. They call that the sculptor's degree of vision." Remington laughed . . . but it started him thinking.

It was apparently the noted sculptor Frederic W. Ruckstull who was really responsi-

* Augustus Thomas, *The Print of My Remembrance*, p. 327.

PORTRAIT SKETCHES
From "Drawings"
The lower left a self-portrait of Remington not previously published

ble for Remington's first attempt at sculpturing. A tent had been set up on a vacant lot not far from the Remington home in New Rochelle, in the summer of 1895, and in it Ruckstull began the half-size clay model of his heroic equestrian statue of Brigadier General John F. Hartranft which stands on Capitol Hill, Harrisburg, Pennsylvania. Remington met Ruckstull and visited the tent where he was working—his first intimate view of a sculptor at work. The horse particularly attracted him; and he became interested. The following account is from the unpublished memoirs of the sculptor, which were completed just before his death on May 26, 1942:

"Within a mile radius [in New Rochelle] there were a number of artists who used to foregather at the Augustus Thomas's—Francis Wilson, the actor; Ed Kemble, the illustrator; Zogbaum, also illustrator; Ernest Albert, painter. These and many others would come in of Saturday or Sunday evenings, bringing friends from all over the world. And there was Frederic Remington, the 'all-round artist' who lived close by and who ran in frequently, at all hours, to rout out Thomas and me for a tramp or a bicycle ride. He became very much intrigued by the Hartranft model I was making.

"One Sunday morning I was loafing with him in his studio. 'Ruck,' he said suddenly, 'do you think I could model? Thomas has suggested that I could.' 'Certainly you can.' 'What makes you say certainly?' he asked. 'Because you *see*, in your mind, so very clearly anything that you want to draw. You will be able to draw just as clearly in wax as you do on paper.' 'But how about the technique of it?' he queried with a quizzical look. 'Technique be hanged,' I replied. 'Forget it and it will take care of itself. Then you will have an individual technique, or surface modelling, personal and peculiar to you, and in this epoch of a craze for individuality that will be an added quality. All you need to think of is a popular subject, a fine composition, correct movement and expressive form. Begin right away. You can do it. Take that drawing of yours of a Bronco Buster—you can start with that. I'll get a modelling stand, and tools and modelling wax for you, and show you how to make a wire skeleton for supporting the wax, and all that.' He jumped up eagerly. 'By God!' he exclaimed boyishly, 'I can try anyhow, can't I?' 'And you can't fail,' I replied.

"I went to New York, ordered all the paraphernalia he needed, and soon he was busy as a bee modelling and producing his 'Bronco Buster.' "

"The Bronco Buster" which he chose for his first attempt was not an easy subject. It presented technical problems that would have daunted many a sculptor of wide experience. To produce balance and grace, and at the same time realism, in standing a bucking bronco on his hind legs, with a rider on his back, proved exceedingly difficult, but his determination carried him through to the task's completion. Nor did he seek or receive any advice or assistance. As a matter of fact, he had such difficulty that he very nearly decided not to have the finished model cast in bronze, which might have ended his career as a sculptor. Only the encouragement and insistence of some close friend (probably Augustus Thomas) saved the now famous "Bronco Buster." It was copyrighted on October 1, 1895; and here is Remington's description as written in his own hand on the application for copyright: "Equestrian statue of cowboy mounted upon and breaking in wild horse standing on hind feet. Cowboy holding onto horse's mane with left hand while right hand is extended upwards."

Almost immediately the "Bronco Buster" was accepted as art worthy of high acclaim. In one leap Remington had won what proved to be lasting renown as a sculptor—although he was more purely self-taught in this difficult branch of the arts than in any other.

On October 19, 1895, within less than three weeks after it was copyrighted, *Harper's Weekly* devoted a full page to the "Bronco Buster." This included a large photograph and a highly complimentary review by Arthur Hoeber, the noted contemporary critic, a part of which is given here:

"The 'Bronco Buster,' with its spirited action of horse and rider, presents no easy problem. Mr. Remington has, however, solved it satisfactorily. Every detail has been carried out, from the Rarey hitch about the animal's head to the hide flaps flying back from the man's legs. The action is stirring, though not forced, and the sculptor has seized all the possibilities of the situation with rare judgment. . . . He has handled his clay in a masterly way, with great freedom and certainty of touch, and in a manner to call forth the surprise and admiration not only of his fellow craftsmen, but of sculptors as well. Mr. Remington has struck his gait, and that, much as he has accomplished in an illustrative way, more remains for him to do, and other roads are open to him. With youth, health and energy, who shall say how far he may not go? And his is a distinctly American field."

Remington's own quite typical comment was: "I have always had a feeling for mud, and I did that [the Bronco Buster]—a long work attended with great difficulty on my part. I wanted to do something which a burglar wouldn't have, moths eat, or time blacken. It [sculpture] is a great art and satisfying to me, for my whole feeling is for form."

As an indication of the ultimate success of this first sculpture, it may be noted that the 250 bronze copies of the "Bronco Buster," which were cast before the model was destroyed, sold for a total of $62,500. A considerable number more of these bronzes might have been sold, but he limited the number made; and a very few, possibly not more than one or two, were cast in silver. Today these bronzes are even more popular than they were when they were new, and they appear on the open market at as much as six times their original sales price. Fake reproductions of the "Bronco Buster" also abound—an offensive gesture of acclaim toward its creator.

Encouraged by his initial success in the field of sculpturing, Remington was soon working on a second hunk of clay, which became "The Wounded Bunkie" copyrighted on July 9, 1896, or little more than nine months after the "Bronco Buster." This also was a Western equestrian subject, and of considerably more ambitious composition. The two horses are in full gallop, side by side, with only a single hoof of each animal touching the ground. Each horse carries a frontier cavalryman, one of whom has been wounded and is supported in his saddle by the strong arm of the other trooper who has come alongside just in time to save this "wounded bunkie" from falling. The action of both horses is superb, particularly the one carrying the trooper whose unconscious hand has just lost its grip on the rein. From whatever angle the group is viewed, the composition produces a particularly pleasing impression and feeling of galloping speed. This bronze is today much sought after, since only fourteen copies were cast for the artist.

Remington did not abandon his drawing, painting or writing, for sculpturing. It was just a new medium added to his intensive work. Pen-and-ink, wash, oil in black and white or color, pastel and even etching were all now handled with equal facility, as well as fiction and fact in his writing; and he could turn from any one to any of the others without the slightest evidence of difficulty or effort. He would work hard at painting through part of a day and then turn to sculpturing as a form of relaxation and rest—or vice versa. He generally had more than one picture in progress at the same time—sometimes several—apparently for the same purpose.

To continue the story of Remington's sculpturing, his third bronze was "The Wicked Pony," sometimes called "The Fallen Rider," which was copyrighted December 3, 1898; and "The Scalp," sometimes referred to as "The Triumph," was copyrighted on December 10, 1898. "The Wicked Pony" shows a cowboy who has been thrown and is lying flat on the ground. The bronco, entering into the situation in true Western style, is lashing out with his hind legs. It is said that the inspiration for this was an actual incident, in which the bronco killed its rider—hence the title. The other subject, "The Scalp," represents an Indian reining up his horse as he triumphantly holds aloft a scalp which he has taken from a defeated enemy.

In 1901 Frederic Remington's sculpturing showed a sudden and definite improvement. This was not the result of any new skill, but was owing to the particular method by which his clay models were cast into bronze. Remington was one of the first sculptors in the United States to have his statues reproduced by the *cire perdue* (lost wax) process—the method by which Cellini and other of the early Italian masters cast their work. The man who was directly responsible for this, and who through the years that followed played an important rôle in assisting Remington to achieve such high degree of perfection in the casting of his statues, is Riccardo Bertelli.

Before Bertelli set up his Roman Bronze Works, in a studio opposite the Metropolitan Opera House, Remington had had his casting done by Henry-Bonnard where the "sand" method was used. The difference in quality between the earlier and later castings is remarkable. Bertelli and Remington became fast friends, and Bertelli still chuckles over the artist's idiosyncrasies and frequent displays of temperament.

"He always wanted to have his horses with all four feet *off* the ground," Bertelli said in a recent conversation with this writer. "I sometimes had quite a time with him. Once he sent me a Christmas card which he had sketched. It showed a caricature of himself beside a modelling stand on which was the clay model of a bucking horse precariously balanced on the tip of one toe, like a ballerina. Underneath the sketch he wrote: 'Can you cast him?' And below was my imagined reply, 'Do you think I am one of the Wright Brothers?' "

Up to the end of 1900 Remington had done only five pieces of sculpture. In the nine years that followed, however, he completed seventeen more with variations of three subjects. He did a total of twenty-five bronzes.

He completed "The Cheyenne" (a variant of which was later made) and "The Buffalo Signal" in 1901; and in 1902 he produced his famous "Coming Through the Rye" or "Off the Range" as it is sometimes called. The last represents four cowboys mounted on broncos dashing at full gallop, waving their six-shooters over their heads with quirts flying from their wrists. They have the spark of abandon and deviltry in their hollow eyes; and their mouths are open as though in the act of shrieking out some wild Western apostrophe to the red gods of recklessness. The broncos, snorting and straining forward, are shoulder to shoulder, and their flying hoofs emphasize the devil-may-care of such a mad ride. With the exception of "The Bronco Buster" (a larger version of which he made in 1905) "Coming Through the Rye" is the best known and most popular of Remington's bronzes. A heroic plaster replica of this sculpture was exhibited at the St. Louis (Louisiana Purchase) Exhibition in 1904, and was also placed at the head of Columbia Court, the main plaza of the Lewis and Clark Exposition at Portland, Oregon, in 1905. Copies of the original bronze are today keenly sought by museums and art collectors.

Remington assisted Bertelli in the actual casting of his bronzes; and sometimes, with the more difficult subjects, his temperament almost ended the existence of the model. On one occasion, when they were having trouble in getting the casting of "Coming Through the Rye" to come out as desired, he suddenly picked up a metal bar and slammed it down on the model. Fortunately Bertelli restrained him, but not until considerable damage had been done which had to be carefully repaired before further castings could be made.

In his bronzes, as in all his other forms of work, Remington was strictly a realist and never would he compromise fact or reality for art or composition. An instance of this occurred during the preliminary negotiations which resulted in his doing "The Fairmount Park Cowboy"—a heroic equestrian statue of a cowboy on a Spanish horse, which was unveiled in Fairmount Park, Philadelphia, on June 20, 1908. He had, at the time of this incident, submitted a small model and was called to Philadelphia to consult with the City Fathers. Riccardo Bertelli accompanied him.

"Mr. Remington," said one dignified old gentleman, when they had gathered in the large consultation room where Remington's small model stood in the center of a great table, "we like the model you have submitted and have about decided to commission you to do the statue. There are, however, one or two points we want to discuss. . . ." Then he explained, among other things, that from the standpoint of artistic symmetry the horse's front foot was wrong. Remington had made the toe of the extended hoof point straight out (even a little upward); and the city's art experts wanted it curved more gracefully downward.

"What the hell do you know about horses!" boomed Remington, hardly waiting for the last words and jumping to his feet as if quite prepared to depart then and there with his model under his arm.

Bertelli managed to calm him down and soothe the injured feelings of the shocked City Fathers, and Remington got the job. But the big bronze horse which stands in Fairmount Park has the tip of its extended hoof pointing straight out—and even a little upward. No considerations of profit could ever induce Remington to compromise with the truth about the noble animal he knew and loved as well as any man who ever lived.

"That," explained Bertelli, "is the fundamental difference between Remington's work and the statuary of those who have given more consideration to art than realism."

Examples of Remington's work in sculpture are to be found in many of the country's most discriminating art museums, such as The Metropolitan Museum of Art in New York, the Corcoran Gallery in Washington, D. C., Detroit Institute of Arts, and others. But the Remington bronzes, like his pictures, are also to be found displayed in public places far removed from the dignified galleries of art museums—as, for example, in Jack Kelly's Saloon in Hoboken, New Jersey, and the "21" Club in New York City.

In Remington's work as a sculptor, just as in his work as an artist, his subjects are the unheralded people of the land and the soil, and not the glamorously publicized personalities, such as Buffalo Bill, General Miles or Sitting Bull. For him to have done a bust of Theodore Roosevelt as leader of the Rough Riders would have given Remington considerable prestige and profit; but instead he chose to devote his time and skill to perpetuating the unnamed cowboys, troopers and Indians.

CHAPTER XIV

War Correspondent Under Fire

OR years Remington had harbored a desire to portray scenes of a large-scale modern war, involving the participation of extensive troops, artillery and great columns of cavalry—the sort of thing done by some of the French artists whose work had impressed him as a youth. He could easily have fabricated fanciful pictures of almost any of the great battles or cavalry charges of history, but Remington was not that kind of an artist. The prerequisite was firsthand observation.

Early on the morning of February sixteenth, 1898, Augustus Thomas telephoned Remington with some exciting news. "James Waterbury, the Western Union agent, just telephoned me that the U.S. battleship *Maine* has been blown up and sunk in Havana Harbor. It means war!"

"Ring off!" Remington interrupted bruskly, and before the line was clear he was frantically trying to get through to the editor of *Harper's Weekly* in New York. This was his chance to see a war, and he was going to lose no time in getting into it.

In an amazingly short time, he was on his way to Key West, representing not only *Harper's* but also Hearst's New York *Journal* and newspaper syndicate. There is a story that Hearst wired Remington: "You supply the pictures and I'll supply the war." He and Richard Harding Davis were to try to sneak into Cuba "by the back door" before our troops landed, an assignment exactly suited to their differing but congenial temperaments.

In Key West, they engaged a fast boat to land under cover of night on the shore of Cuba, but storms and high seas twice forced them to turn back. On the third attempt, even the crew abandoned hope of getting safely back to Key West; and any idea of reaching Cuba was blown away on the screaming wind. Remington and Davis lay in the scuppers hanging on for dear life to keep from being washed overboard by the high seas that swept the deck. The Chinese cook was struggling to lash together a life raft out of a door and some boxes, and Davis suggested that they might well do the same for themselves. "Lie still," Remington ordered. "I've been watching him. You and I don't know how to do that sort of thing. Let him make his raft. If we capsize I'll throttle that Chinaman and we'll take the raft." Fortunately, his sense of self-preservation was not taxed that far, and the boat limped back into Key West. The two correspondents decided to go in with the troops. . . .

Aboard the battleship *Iowa*, Remington spent seven long days and sultry nights steaming along the Cuban coast while the fortifications were bombarded. But this was much too mild for him. "I want," he wrote, "to hear a 'shave-tail' bawl; I want to get some dust in my throat; kick dewy grass; to see a sentry in the moonlight; and to talk the language of my tribe."*

When he learned that the port of embarkation for our troops was Tampa, Florida, he hurried there and made arrangements to go with the first contingent.

"Now it is so arranged in the world that I hate a ship in a compound, triple-expansion, forced-draught way," he wrote in *Harper's Monthly*.† "Do anything to me, but do not have me entered on the list of a ship. It does not matter if I am to be the lordly proprietor of the finest yacht afloat, make me a feather in a sick chicken's tail on shore, and I will thank you. So it came about that I did an unusual amount of real suffering in consequence of living on the *Seguança* during the long voyage to Cuba."

Remington's ship was one of those that lay close in the wake of Sampson's fleet as it ran close in on Daiquiri Bay and "turned everything loose" on the chosen landing place. He watched Navy launches tow in the long lines of landing boats crowded with soldiery; and the horses and mules being thrown overboard to make shore under their own power—for this was the general plan followed for storming and establishing the first beach-head on Cuba in '98. And as soon as the American flag was seen hoisted over the Spanish blockhouse atop the steep hill, the correspondents were put ashore.

With three days' supply of crackers, coffee and pork, a canteen, rubber poncho, sketch pads and six-shooter, Remington hit the beach and moved out with the Sixth Cavalry on the first afternoon of the Spanish-American War on the soil of Cuba.

"I sat on a hill," his account in *Harper's Monthly* continues, "and down in the road below saw the long line of troops pressing up the valley toward Siboney. When our troops got on the beach, each soldier adjusted his roll, shouldered his rifle and started for Santiago, apparently by individual intuition. . . . I think our army would never have stopped until it cracked into the doomed city in column formation, if Shafter had not discovered this unlooked-for enterprise and sent his personal aide on a fast horse with positive orders to halt until the 'cracker line' could be fixed up behind them."

* "Wigwags from the Blockade," *Harper's Weekly*, May 14, 1898.
† "With the Fifth Corps," *Harper's Monthly*, Nov., 1898.

QUESTIONABLE COMPANIONSHIP.
Harper's Weekly, August 9, 1890.

The following morning, finding the Sixth Cavalry still tied down waiting orders to advance, Remington shouldered his "little hotel equipment" and started out alone to find the "front."

Sweating under the stifling heat he made his way slowly along the jungle road, the sides of which were already cluttered with castoff blue uniforms, coats, overcoats and gray blankets left just where the soldiers had got up from them after the first night's rest. He stopped to crack open coconuts to drink the milk; saw Cubans in the clothing of Spanish soldiers killed by our troops; and by nightfall he "lay up beside the road outside of Siboney, cooked supper by a soldier fire, and lay down under a mango tree on the rubber poncho, with the haversack for a pillow."

At Siboney he fell in with John Fox, fellow-correspondent and writer, and together they moved forward to see the fighting. But then it began to rain; and "at evening, after we had 'bummed' some crackers and coffee from some good-natured officer, we repaired to our neck of the woods and stood gazing at our musty bed. It was good, soft, soggy mud; and on it, or rather in it, we laid one of our ponchos, and over that spread the other."

At last Remington had the good fortune to buy a horse from an officer who had been wounded and was going to the rear. And finally he reached the place where Capron's battery was just laying its guns to begin shelling the stone fort on El Caney Hill.

For a while Remington watched the battery knock holes in the Spanish stronghold and our infantry exchange brisk rifle fire, from the jungle, with the enemy in their trenches below the fort.

Learning that there was a large movement of troops and guns toward Santiago, and surmising that that would be the "big show," Remington worked his way down to the main road.

"Sure enough," he writes, "the road was jammed with troops; up El Paso Hill went the horses of Grimes's battery under whip and spur . . . and along the road stood the Rough Riders—Roosevelt's now, for Wood was a brigadier. Grimes fired a few shells toward Santiago, and directly came a screaming shrapnel from the Spanish lines. It burst over the Rough Riders, and the manoeuver picture on the hill underwent a lively change. It was thoroughly evident the Spaniards had the range of everything in the country. For myself, I fled, dragging my horse up the hill. Some as gallant soldiers, and as daring correspondents as it is my pleasure to know, did their legs proud there. The tall form of Major John Jacob Astor moved in my front in jack-rabbit bounds. Directly came the warning scream of No. 2, and we dropped, and hugged the ground like star-fish. Bang! right over us it exploded. The next shell went into the battery, killing and doing damage. Following shells were going into the troops down in the road.

"As I wormed my way up the fateful road toward Santiago, fellows I knew out West and up North and down South passed their word to me and I felt that I was not alone. A shrapnel came shrieking down the road, and I got a drink of water and a cracker from Colonel Garlington. The column of troops was working its way into battle-line. I could hear noises such as you can make if you strike quickly with a small walking-stick at a very few green leaves. Some of them were very near and others more faint. They were the Mausers, and out in front through the jungle I could hear what sounded like Fourth of July morning. It struck me as new, strange, almost uncanny, because I wanted the roar of battle.

"Then came the light as I passed out of the jungle, and forded San Juan River. The clicking in the leaves continued, and the fire-crackers rattled out in front.

" 'Get down, old man; you'll catch one,' said an old alkali friend, and I got down, sitting there with the officers of the cavalry brigade. Promptly some surgeons came along, saying it was the only safe place, and they began to dig the sand to level it. We, in consequence, moved out into the crackle, and I tied my horse with some others. 'Too bad, old fellow,' I thought; 'I should have left you behind. Modern rifle fire is rough on horses. They can't get down. But, you dear old thing, you will have to take your chances.' And I then looked at the preparations for the field hospital. A man came, stooping over, with his arms drawn up and hands flapping downward at the wrists—that's the way with all people when they are shot through the body.

"Then the oncoming troops poured through the hole in the jungle which led to San Juan Hill. As the troops came pouring across the ford they stooped as low as they anatomically could, and their faces were wild with excitement. The older officers stood up as straight as on parade. They may have done it through pride, or they may have known that it is better to be 'drilled clean' than to have a long-ranging wound. It was probably both.

"Then came a curious old tube drawn by a big mule, and Borrowe with his Rough Riders. It was the dynamite gun. The mule was unhooked and turned loose. The gun was trundled up the road and laid for a shot. The poor old mule lay down with a grunt and slowly died. The fire was now incessant. The horses lay down, one after another, as the Mausers found their billets. I tried to take mine to a place of safety, but a sharp-shooter potted at me, and I gave up. There was no place of safety.

"Now men came walking or were carried into the temporary hospital in a string. One boy was brought in by two tough hairy old soldiers, his head hanging down behind. His shirt was off, and a big red spot shone brilliantly against his marble skin. They laid him tenderly down, and the surgeon stooped over him. The doctor folded his arms across his breast and turned to a man who held a wounded foot up to him, dumbly imploring aid, as a dog might.

"I went down the creek, keeping under the bank and then out into the 'scrub,' hunting for our line. The bullets cut and clicked around, and a sharp-shooter nearly did me. I ran quickly across a space. 'Wheet!' came a Mauser, and it was right next to my ear, and two more. I dropped in the tall guinea-grass, and crawled to some soldiers, hidden under a mango tree. I think that episode cost me my sketch book. I believe I lost it during that crawl, and the Spaniard shot so well I wouldn't trust him again.

"From the vantage of a little bank under a big tree I had my first glimpse of San Juan Hill—and the bullets whistled about. Our men out in front were firing. I had no idea that they were to assault that hill. I did not understand how our men could stay out there under the gruelling fire. Directly I heard our line yelling, and even then did not suppose it was an assault. Then the Mausers came in continuous whistle.

"I crawled along to a new place and finally got sight of the fort, and just then I could see our blue soldiers on the hill top—and I also noticed that the Mauser bullets rained no more. Then I started after.

"The country was alive with wounded men—some to die in the dreary jungle, some to get their happy home-draft, but all to be miserable. Only a handful of men got to the top, where they broke out a flag and cheered. 'Cheer' is the word for that sound. You have got to hear it once where it means so much, and ever after you will thrill when Americans make that noise.

"San Juan was taken by infantry and dismounted cavalry of the United States regular army without the aid of artillery. It was a most glorious feat of arms, considering every condition. It was done without grub, without reserves of either ammunition or men, and under tropical conditions. It was a storm of intrenched heights, held by veteran troops armed with modern guns, supported by artillery, and no other troops on the earth would have even thought that they could take San Juan heights, let alone doing it."

Remington stood on San Juan Hill with our troops who stormed and took the famous Spanish stronghold on the way to Santiago; and he remained through the desperate counterattack which the hurriedly reorganized enemy made in an unsuccessful attempt to re-take that strategic point.

Having had nothing whatever to eat during the entire day, and little more than Army crackers and muddy water for several days, he made his way back to headquarters camp. He found his horse unharmed, one of the three animals which escaped death at San Juan ford. The fever, which took greater toll of men and officers than did the enemy's bullets, now struck Remington also. He tried to fight it off and return to the front, but he could get no farther than El Paso Hill.

For an entire day he lay on the ground in the intense heat, staggering to his feet only to drink deeply and unwisely of the dirty water that ran in a near-by creek. His fever-dulled eyes watched the re-enforcements marching slowly toward the front; the

102

sound of shells railroading down through the jungle could hardly be distinguished from the constant pounding in his head. As the day came to a close, he roused sufficiently to realize that his part in this campaign was finished, and he joined the "broken spirits, bloody bodies, hopeless, helpless, suffering which drags its weary way to the rear." With the other sick and wounded, he was returned to the United States, where his vitality reasserted itself and he soon recovered.

For Remington, as for many other participants, the Spanish-American War had not been a particularly inspiring or satisfactory experience. Yet out of it came several important war pictures by this artist. Among them is one painting that is unique in Remingtoniana. His "Charge of the Rough Riders at San Juan Hill,"‡ is the only occasion, so far as we know, when Remington put his art to the service of politics.

His dislike for politics and politicians was intense and outspoken; and with exceedingly rare exceptions his subjects were anonymous types, not personalities such as Theodore Roosevelt. The two men, however, had been friends for more than ten years. Roosevelt's encouragement had meant a great deal when Remington was a young unknown, and Remington had a sincere respect for him as a man, whether or not he sympathized with him as a politician. But now Roosevelt was facing a very critical point in his own career and he could use some assistance such as Remington was in a position to give. Roosevelt was being groomed for the New York State gubernatorial campaign, as a stepping-stone to bigger and more important political horizons. The claim that Remington's painting of Teddy Roosevelt leading his Rough Riders in a dramatic charge up San Juan Hill helped to put his old friend in the White House is no exaggeration, for it certainly played a part in creating the legend of "T. R." as a soldier. Colored reprints were widely circulated, lending credence to Richard Harding Davis's dramatic and romantic news dispatches which also contributed to the heroic legend. And as indication that there was some inspiration behind the painting of this particular picture, other than putting paint on canvas to document the war, it can be observed that the picture was never used for either *Harper's* or Hearst's *Journal*, for whom Remington was working under contract; and it is now pretty well established that the artist never saw Roosevelt lead such a charge up San Juan Hill. The picture was, however, used as an illustration for Theodore Roosevelt's own account of the Spanish-American War, in "The Rough Riders" which appeared in *Scribner's Magazine*, January-June 1899. The original painting, which is somewhat larger than most of Remington's canvases, now hangs in the Remington Art Memorial at Ogdensburg.

When the famous Rough Riders were disbanded at Montauk, Long Island, after returning from the war in Cuba, they presented their leader, Colonel Theodore Roosevelt, with a bronze casting of Remington's "Bronco Buster" as a parting gift. Standing beside a small table on which the bronze had been placed, the great Teddy shook

‡ Reproduced in *Scribner's Magazine*, April 1899.

hands with each of his men as they filed past. Shortly afterward, in a letter sent to Remington from Oyster Bay, under date of September 10, 1898, he wrote: "It was the most appropriate gift the Regiment could possibly have given me and the one I would have valued most. I have long looked hungrily at that bronze, but to have it come to me in this precise way seemed almost too good." In reply, Remington wrote that it made him "very proud that the Rough Riders had put their brand on my Bronco Buster."

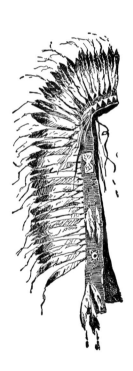

CHAPTER XV

The Squire of Ingleneuk

As he approached forty, Remington's girth and avoirdupois continued to increase, a fact which failed to deter him from consuming four to six lamb chops or a liberal helping of pigs' knuckles at breakfast with three huge cups of coffee and many sundry side issues. Riding was now practically a thing of the past, but he was still a mighty swimmer, played a ferocious game of tennis and ping-pong, and lived up to his theory that "every man should get up a real sweat at least once a day."

His regular trips to the West were less arduous than they had been, but then the West itself was changing, losing much of the spectacular, dramatic quality he loved and the remnants of which he had sought to record before they disappeared altogether. When Remington spoke of the West, it was generally as "my West," and there was sorrow in his voice as he mourned its passing.

"The West is no longer the West of picturesque and stirring events," he said. "Romance and adventure have been beaten down in the rush of civilization. The country west of the Mississippi has become hopelessly commercialized, shackled in the chains of business, to its uttermost limits. The cowboy—the real thing, mark you, not the tame hired man who herds cattle for the mere wage of it, and who lives for weeks at a time in conventional store clothes—disappeared with the advent of the wire fence. As for the Indian, there are so few of him that he doesn't count; besides, he has gone into trade, into politics, into real estate, and is sending his children to Eastern schools and colleges to learn how he may best outwit the white man's law. I have no interest in the industrial West of today—no more interest than I have in the agriculture of East Prussia, or the coal mines of Wales. My West passed utterly out of existence so long ago as to make it merely a dream. It took off its blankets, put on its hat and marched off the board; the curtain came down and a new act was in progress."

Eastern-born men have been known to advertise their passion for the West by the outer trappings of sombreros, cowboy boots, and colored handkerchiefs in place of ties. This had never been Remington's way, perhaps because he was fortunate enough to be able to express his sentiments in a truer, more enduring form. His fondness for good and expensive clothes seldom slid over into the bizarre, though occasionally his taste in neckties called forth jests from his friends, whereupon he would invariably go out and purchase an entire new assortment discarding the old out of hand. And one day, as his sister-in-law recalls, he did come home with a large black sombrero with every apparent intention of wearing it into town. Dressed for the city, he tried the sombrero on in front of a mirror and, ignoring his wife's objections, wore it away. Within a brief time, however, he was back again for another look in the mirror, while Missie again suggested that his derby would be more appropriate. And again he started stubbornly out wearing the big hat, only to return once more, this time sheepishly laying aside the sombrero in favor of the conventional headgear.

The Players was a usual haven for him in New York. There he was sure of finding some of his many friends, good conversation, witty repartee, and the masculine atmosphere he enjoyed. On rare occasion he could be inveigled into attending exhibitions, though the reluctance, amounting almost to a phobia, to study the work of other artists had not diminished with time.

"You didn't seem very enthusiastic about the exhibition," a friend remarked as they left a gallery of Impressionistic paintings.

"Enthusiastic!" Remington exploded. "Say, I've got two maiden aunts up-state who can *knit* better pictures than those."

His tendency to rush home right after lunch called forth sarcastic quips at The Players. "Frederic's going home to milk the cows," was a favorite gibe. The wish to escape even farther from the city and its crowds and the rapidly growing suburb of New Rochelle in 1898, had much to do with his buying "Ingleneuk," an island in Chippewa Bay on the St. Lawrence River. It was, in a sense, a going-home as well, for this was the same North country of New York State where he had spent his early youth. It was not that Remington was antisocial, although he was always something of a lone wolf, but being a very hard worker he did not like to be disturbed.

The stony, grass-covered island in the St. Lawrence, about five acres in area, studded with a picturesque growth of white birch, beech and pine, had a bold rocky shore with a small bay, fringed with white sand, on the lee side. About three miles of blue water stretched northward to Canada, and a narrow neck of water separated it from its nearest island neighbor. He made additions to the fairly large house already there, built a separate studio near by, made a tennis court and otherwise improved the place. Eva Remington herself painted the library, living room and four upstairs bedrooms, the latter in pleasant colors of lavender, green, pink and blue. There were to be many

BRONCO BUSTERS SADDLING
Century, February 1888

A CALIFORNIA CART
Century, December 1890

guests, for Remington's dislike of "civilization" never extended to a burning desire for solitude.

During at least part of the ten summers after 1898 Remington lived at "Ingleneuk," painting and writing with furious energy, loving every inch of his little feudal kingdom and all the waters around it. He scoffed at rowboats, sailboats and motorboats, saying he would "just as soon ride on a street car," but when he was not working he could almost always be found in his canoe, wandering alone over the rippling St. Lawrence and up the wild creeks that wound back through the woodlands flanking the shore. The fragile craft sank deeply in the water under his enormous weight, but that did not bother him at all. Once he bought a gasoline launch but after a couple of trips during which the engine behaved with all the recalcitrance a gasoline engine is capable of, he tied it up to the dock and relieved his fury by hurling rocks and tools at the thing.

"Ingleneuk" one year suffered from a superfluity of toads and Remington hired some of the local boys to catch and transport them unharmed to the mainland where they were to be liberated, paying the boys five cents for every toad they captured. The boys, who grew up to be successful businessmen of Ogdensburg, got ideas. Instead of releasing the toads on the mainland, they kept them in a box for a few days. Then they went back to "Ingleneuk" and, under the pretense of catching more, collected five cents apiece for the same toads. "Why, some of those toads we must have sold to Remington at least five or six times!" laughed one of the perpetrators many years afterward. If Remington ever guessed their ruse, he never let the boys know it.

The same boys were put to work one spring doing some repair work on the dock, which meant spending a large part of their time in the icy water. Eventually Remington wandered down from the house and found all labor suspended while the boys sat in the sun shivering.

"Hell, you boys are a bunch of sissies!" he threw at them scornfully.

One of them apologized through chattering teeth. "That water's almighty cold, Mr. Remington."

Although he was dressed in white flannels, Remington promptly walked to the end of the dock and with a derisive laugh jumped into the deep water. He came up with an astonished look on his face and clambered back onto the dock a good deal faster than he had gone in.

"You're right!" he admitted with a chuckle. "That water's *damned* cold. Come on up to the house and have something to eat while you get warm."

His routine at "Ingleneuk" was the same as in New Rochelle: up at six, turn on the phonograph full blast, breakfast at seven sharp, then to work; only varied by an occasional expedition to bring in fish for the morning meal, and in the afternoon swimming, tennis or canoeing.

108

During all his years at "Ingleneuk," as well as New Rochelle, his production of magazine writing was amazingly large considering the quantity of work he was doing in other fields. Writing was, he confessed, always difficult for him; it did not come spontaneously as had sculpture. But he had been writing almost as long as he had been illustrating, mostly journalistic accounts of his experiences and reporting on events he witnessed, but it was good writing—good enough for the best popular magazines of the day. A considerable number of these articles had been put together and published in book form. *Pony Tracks* had been the first of these, appearing in 1895. Then there was *A Rogers Ranger in the French and Indian War*, in 1897, a twelve-page reprint of his single article "Joshua Goodenough's Old Letter," which appeared in *Harper's Monthly*, November 1897. This latter is, incidentally, the scarcest of all the Remington books. *Crooked Trails*, another group of selected articles that had appeared in *Harper's*, was published in 1898. In the interim, however, his fiction had begun appearing. "The Great Medicine-Horse," which appeared in *Harper's Monthly* in September 1897, and "Massai's Crooked Trail" which came out in the same magazine in January 1898, received high commendation and comparison with the writing of Owen Wister. Into the former of these two stories Remington wove a character whom he called "Sun-Down Leflare." This Western personage began making quite regular appearances as the leading character in subsequent magazine stories, which, on January 4, 1899, formed the basis for Remington's fourth book. *Sun-Down Leflare* marked another important step in its author's career—from fact to fiction, as a writer.

After reading "Massai's Crooked Trail," Theodore Roosevelt, then Assistant Secretary of the Navy, wrote the author: "Are you aware, O sea-going plainsman, that aside from what you do with the pencil, you come closer to the real thing with the pen than any other man in the western business? And I include Hough, Grinnell and Wister. Your articles have been a growing surprise. . . . Somehow you get close not only to the plainsman and soldier, but to the halfbreed and Indian, in the same way Kipling does to the British Tommy and the Gloucester codfisher. Literally, innumerable short stories and sketches of cowboys, Indians and soldiers have been, and will be written. . . . The very best will live and will make the cantos in the last epic of the Western Wilderness, before it ceased being a wilderness. Now, I think you are writing this 'very best.' "

October 10, 1899, saw the publication of *Stories of Peace and War*; and less than four months later, on January 30, 1900, *Men With the Bark On* made its appearance. Six books in less than five years is an enviable record even for a writer with no other vocational interest. None of his books brought Remington either fame or money to compare with his illustrations, painting and sculpture, but they were received with praise and attained a pleasant measure of popularity.

In estimating Remington's success as a writer, it must be remembered that he faced extraordinary competition. A famous school of Western writers were then in their prime—such men as Owen Wister, Bret Harte, Alfred Henry Lewis, Joaquin Miller, Stewart Edward White. Remington had illustrated stories by some of them and was thoroughly familiar with their work. One cannot easily withhold admiration for a man who, already established and even famous in one field, branches out into another which is crowded with masterly workmen. Remington brought to writing the instinctive feeling for color and form, the freshness and vitality and faithfulness to realistic detail that mark his pictures and bronzes. Actually, his fiction and nonfiction simply gave him another medium for expounding the story he had set himself to tell—the story of our Old West.

In 1902 Remington turned to the writing of fiction with real seriousness. After considerable planning and forethought he decided to lay aside both his painting and sculpturing and devote the summer at "Ingleneuk" to writing a Western novel. It was to be a frontier romance, woven around a glamorous young white man who had been raised from early childhood by an old Indian trapper. Of unknown white parents, this individual grew up to be more red man than white, in spite of his golden hair. But when he became a scout for the U. S. Army in its campaign against his foster-parent's tribal enemies the Sioux, and fell in love with the Army Major's beautiful daughter— then the story, and the tragedy, unfolds. Remington chose to call his hero "John Ermine of the Yellowstone." It was the most difficult writing task he had undertaken, and the joy with which he completed the work is told by Edwin Wildman,* one of Remington's summer neighbors:

" 'Come down here; I want to speak to you,' Remington called one day, shoving the nose of his canoe up against my dock. 'I've coined two words today—the sweetest ones in the English language.' I leaned over the dock, watching the beatific smile that played upon his boyish features. 'Bend low. I want to whisper them to you.' I craned my neck forward as he grasped my arm and whooped out: 'T-H-E E-N-D!' Then he paddled merrily away and went on a holiday."

Just before sunset, the day before he left for his home in New Rochelle, Remington paddled out in the bay, back of his island, and painted a sketch of his boathouse and the white rocks and green trees that line the shore.

" 'First time I've touched the brush this summer,' " he later told Wildman. " 'Got to take some of the light and water home with me to look at this winter.† Just live to come up here—can't beat it anywhere. You want to get away from everything to catch the spirit of the out-of-doors—away from houses and people's gabble. White man tries to spoil nature by trying to improve on it. The march of the derby hat round the world is answerable for more crimes against art than a hundred wars.

* *Outing Magazine*, Mar., 1903.
† These sketches are now in the Remington Art Memorial, Ogdensburg, N. Y.

" 'Seems as if I *must* paint them—' he continued, admiring the sunset as the colors took on more beautiful hues over the St. Lawrence. 'Seems as if they'd never be so beautiful again. But people won't stand for my painting sunsets,' he added, exploding with a laugh that shook the boat. 'Got me pigeonholed in their minds, you see; want horses, cowboys, out-West things—won't believe me if I paint anything else. . . .' "

The book *John Ermine of the Yellowstone* was published November 12, 1902. It was well received, although it did not make any of the best-seller lists.

John Ermine also became a play. It was adapted for the stage by the well-known playwright Louis Evan Shipman. James K. Hackett produced it and starred in the leading masculine rôle, with Charlotte Walker in the feminine lead. The first public presentation served as the formal opening of the new Globe Theatre, Weber and Field's playhouse, in Boston, on the night of September 14, 1903, and played to a packed house including the Governor of Massachusetts and members of his staff. The audience was enthusiastic and the reviews generally favorable though most of them were critical of the tragic ending. Two months later, somewhat revised, *John Ermine* was brought to New York, where it played a none too successful engagement at the Manhattan Theatre. It was not a financially profitable venture, Remington believed, because of the public's apathy toward Indians and halfbreeds.

CHAPTER XVI

Art for Art's Sake

R EMINGTON lived and worked on a big scale always. He worked at a pace that would have killed most men; his abilities were great and astonishingly varied; he had become one of the highest-paid illustrators in the world, one of our most popular sculptors and a writer whom many of the best minds praised most highly; and he lived right up to the limit of his income, sometimes going beyond it. And yet he was an artistic radical and strictly a realist. There was no premium attractive enough to cause him to make any compromise to composition, decorativeness, or easy acceptance through popular appeal; no inducement which might cause him to fake an action of man or horse, glamorize or bastardize a costume, or add any touch of theatrics to any scene. And almost entirely the subject matter of his work was the "little man," the anonymous soldier, the unknown Indian, the sweaty cowboy known even among his buddies only as "Jack" or "Jim." When in 1902 a collection of his pictures was published in a folio book titled *Done In The Open*, Owen Wister wrote in the Introduction:

If one asked you to tell what George Washington looked like, you would be able to do so readily. . . . But do you know the look and bearing of the private soldier whom George Washington led to battle? . . . Could you tell how a sergeant looked, as distinguished from a private? . . . How very different an impression . . . has the work of Frederic Remington given us! How well we all know the look of Remington's sergeants, the look of Remington's private! . . . In the generations that follow our own they too will inquire, perhaps, "What did the Continental soldier look like?"—and will never know. And then as they pass down the years, and come to Remington, they will honor and praise him even more than we do now for the imperishable historic work that he has done and is doing. As the historian Green wrote what he called a history of the English people, so Remington is drawing his contemporary history of the most picturesque of the American people. Never until this particular day have we possessed a recorder who should give to posterity the enlisted man to be put alongside with the captain who led him

AN OLD-TIME MOUNTAIN MAN WITH HIS PONIES
Century, January 1889

A PACKER OF MULES
Century, April 1889

A STUDY FROM LIFE
Century, October 1888

into battle. How much more rich the past would be for us if various Remingtons, each in his day, had handed such work down into our sight!

There was something more behind the bringing out of *Done In The Open* than just the publication of a book. It was the same deep motive which had inspired Remington's previous folio book of *Drawings* in 1897, as well as his fine *Bunch of Buckskins* in 1901. He had for a long time wanted to get away from the label of illustrator. To all three books there were introductory notes by Owen Wister, although the plates were left to carry the burden with only the briefest titles. Practically all the pictures had been painted or drawn with the one purpose in mind of being submitted to the public at large on their own merits as pictures alone. They were all "Remington"— without attempt at glamorizing. And there is boldly indicated the artist's underlying ideology that stark realism is more important than decorative beauty. The very first picture in *Drawings*, "Forsythe's Fight on the Republican River, 1868—The Charge of Roman Nose," shows in the foreground at least ten horses that have been killed by Indian arrows, and behind these the remnants of Forsythe's men fighting a desperate defense battle against an overwhelming horde of mounted redskins charging in upon them. It is not a pretty picture. But the historic incident which it portrays truthfully delineates that particular dramatic episode in the struggle to tame the Old West. There is drama in this book—but no melodrama. It is easy to read a whole story in many of the pictures. "An Overland Station: Indians Coming In With The Stage" is a good example. Another is "The Twilight of the Indian." This was Remington's challenge for recognition as artist rather than illustrator.

There are few exceptions to the rule that the painter who would, merely by painting, earn as much as a highly paid illustrator must conform in some degree to the demands of rich patrons. He must meet and bow before the aesthetic standards of his day. Neither of these would Remington consent to do. Yet he admittedly hoped that the National Academy of Design would see fit to make him a full member. Between 1887 and 1899, thirteen of his paintings had hung in eight of the Annual and four of the Autumn Exhibitions of the National Academy and he had won two important awards. In 1891 the Academy had made him an Associate. He waited eight years for full recognition and then after 1899 declined to submit any further work to the Academy exhibitions.

Ironically—and yet perhaps naturally enough—it was a magazine that gave him the opportunity to paint as he wanted to and freed him from the restraints of illustration. His first appearance in *Collier's Weekly* was on January 27, 1898, with an article "The Curse of the Wolves in the Northwest," illustrated by a double-page spread. Very soon *Collier's* began running his pictures on full pages and double pages.

After his "sabbatical" season devoted to *John Ermine*, he returned to painting, under an arrangement with *Collier's* which permitted him to follow his own impulse and inspiration. There was no formal contract. In an informal letter dated May 1, 1903, written in the hand and on the personal stationery of Robert C. Collier, their verbal agreement was confirmed, whereby *Collier's Weekly* was "to have the exclusive rights to reproduce your paintings and illustrations for the next four years and the refusal of anything you write." It was further agreed that Remington should supply the equivalent of at least twelve double pages of art work per year, with provision for extra pictures in case of a war and a suggestion for the special publication of portfolios of reproductions of his pictures. The pay was six thousand dollars per year. This was less than Remington had been making as a free-lance illustrator. But all the originals were to be returned to the artist for re-sale; and, most important of all, was the long desired freedom to paint as he pleased which it gave him. From the start, the work that he did for *Collier's* was on a more ambitious scale than most of his previous magazine work.

The first picture under this new arrangement appeared on September 26, 1903. It was "His First Lesson," a double-page plate in full color. Then came "Fight For the Water Hole"; and thereafter the long parade of fine pictures for which the artist is best known today.

Collier's at the time was also publishing such authors and illustrators as A. Conan Doyle, Rudyard Kipling, Charles Dana Gibson, and under the editorial guidance of Robert J. Collier the magazine was rapidly gaining an outstanding position among periodicals.

Remington's prestige was considerably increased through his association with *Collier's*, not only by the opportunity which it gave him to express himself freely and the important display which was given to the full-color reproductions of his pictures, but the magazine also widely advertised in other periodicals the appearance of his work and arranged for the separate full-color printing of many of the best of these in forms suitable for permanent keeping. Framed copies found their way to the walls of rich men's clubs, sawdust-floored saloons, boys' bedrooms and many other places where men had an interest in the wide-open spaces or an appreciation for what the West once stood for. Today these colored reproductions are sought and cherished by many individuals and museums, not only for their artistic and "Western" appeal, but as collector's items.

At the end of the first year of his agreement with the artist, *Collier's* raised the payment for magazine rights to one thousand dollars for each double-page spread. It may have been in connection with this that Mr. Collier went to Ogdensburg where Remington, who was at "Ingleneuk," came to meet him. Remington's old friend, John Howard, realized the importance of the occasion and took the artist in tow. He insisted that Remington stay at Ogdensburg's Century Club until Collier's arrival, giving strict orders to all the attendants that Remington should not be served any liquor until after the business meeting. Remington acquiesced to everything with a laugh, and during the lunch and the long discussion which followed, loudly ordered "plain seltzer water" while the others took their usual drinks. Everything went well, and it was not until some time afterward that Howard learned Remington had made his own arrangements, and that the "plain seltzer water" was in fact half gin.

Exhibitions of the originals of the *Collier's* paintings were held regularly and with considerable success. At one of these John Howard took a fancy to one of the paintings and asked Remington to make him a price. To his surprise, Remington said, "Twenty-five hundred dollars," which was a good deal more than any of the exhibits were expected to bring. When Howard hesitated to commit himself, the artist began to put on pressure to induce him to buy. Howard finally wrote out a check, feeling that his old friend was taking advantage of him and rather uncomfortable about the whole affair. Weeks and months passed by, and still the check did not clear through the bank. "Why the devil don't you deposit that check?" Howard complained. "I have to carry the darn thing over every time I balance my account." Remington promised he would, but not long afterward when they were settling down to enjoy their after-dinner cigars, he got out of his desk a slip of paper which he carefully twisted into a spill and lighted one end with a match. With this he lighted Howard's cigar and then his own, and methodically let it burn down to his fingertips. "There, John," he chuckled, "I've deposited that damn check of yours."

"For a considerable time," wrote Royal Cortissoz,* the distinguished art critic and art editor of the New York *Herald Tribune* since 1891,

> his pictures were invariably marked by a garishness not to be explained alone by the staccato effects of a landscape whelmed in a blaze of sunshine. I have seen paintings of his which were as hard as nails. But then came a change, one of the most interesting noted in some years past by observers of American art. Mr. Remington suddenly drew near to the end of his long pull. He left far behind him the brittleness of the pen drawings which he once had scattered so profusely through magazines and books. His reds and yellows which had blared so mercilessly from his canvases began to take on more of the aspect of nature. Incidentally, the mark of the illustrator disappeared and that of the painter took its place. As though to give his emergence upon a new plane a special character, he brought forward . . . a number of night scenes which expressly challenged attention by their originality and freshness. His picture of "The Gossips" is, I think, one of the handsomest and most convincing Indian studies ever painted.

Having these new horizons brought within his sight had a powerful influence upon Remington. He must have worked with feverish inspiration. He completed one painting after another, with such speed and regularity that their reproductions could appear in *Collier's* at the rate of as many as three or more each month in the year. They were for the most part large-sized oil paintings, lavish in subject matter and

* *Scribner's*, Feb., 1910.

detail. During the first full year of 1904 appeared such now famous titles as "The Pioneers," "The Santa Fe Trade," "The Gathering of the Trappers," "The Emigrants," "A Night Attack on a Government Wagon Train," "The Bell Mare," and others—one after another that would today bring fifteen thousand dollars, and probably more on the open market, and be considered good investments at those prices.

The *Collier's* issue of March 18, 1905, was published as the "Remington Number" and was devoted principally to the artist and his work. Such articles as "Remington— An Appreciation," by Owen Wister; "Remington—The Man and His Work," by Charles Belmont Davis; "Frederic Remington—Sculptor," by James Barnes; and "A Few Words from Mr. Remington," by himself; together with the colorful cover of a half-civilized Indian, a double-page colored plate "Evening on a Canadian Lake," and numerous other pictures and a portrait, all attest to this artist's wide popular appeal and the high distinction which he had won.

CHAPTER XVII

End of the Trail

BY 1909 Frederic Remington had reached the goal which he had set for himself when he began his career. In the forty-eighth and last year of his life, he had "arrived"—without benefit of mimicking any artistic teaching, school or foreign influence; and without benefit of full approval of that haughty oligarchy, the National Academy. Although still relegated to the sophomorish classification of an "Associate," there were other persons beside himself, unbiased and outside the cloistered personnel of the Academy, who had some feeling in the matter. This may be guessed from an editorial comment which appeared in the art critics' magazine, *The Craftsman,* relative to the National Academy's Exhibition of 1909: "Remington is not represented at all, although he is at present one of the most notable American painters and sculptors which the nation can boast. He is, in fact, one of the few men in this country who has created new conditions in our art; and must be reckoned with as one of the revolutionary figures in our art history." The fact that the foregoing clipping was pasted on one of the pages of Remington's personal diary for that year, is an indication that the matter was of personal concern to the artist—although there is no added annotation regarding it, and research has unearthed no comment of peeve or bitterness.

In spite of his bluster and rough mannerisms, Remington was exceedingly sensitive about his work and almost abnormally self-critical. He made a habit of clearing out the studio—burning or otherwise destroying the canvases that had been around, he thought, too long. His attitude toward his early work was one almost of embarrassment—something of past history which his progress had made outmoded and he wanted to forget. In his personal diary under the date of February 8, 1907 is the rather startling entry: "Burned every old canvas in house today—out on the snow. About 75—and there is nothing left but my landscape studies." Many of the destroyed paintings had appeared as important color plates in *Collier's* and among them were a considerable number of his large oil canvases which today would be exceedingly welcome additions to many an art museum or private gallery. Fortunately, many of them had already been reproduced and were not lost entirely.

At the end of his diary for 1908, the year before he died, is another such notation in his own handwriting, enumerating "27 paintings which were burned"—apparently all at one time. This list includes such well-known pictures as "The Santa Fe Trail," "Going to the Rendezvous," the whole "Explorers" Series—of which there were ten paintings in all—except "La Vérendrye." He also destroyed all the pictures of the "Tragedy of the Trees" and "The Buffalo Hunter."

The Remingtons had now lived in the big house on Webster Avenue, New Rochelle, for almost two decades. But it had become somewhat out-of-date in his scheme of things. The locality had become built up and crowded; and many of the artists and other companionable personalities had moved on to establish new colonies of their kind, farther away from the hustle and bustle of Manhattan. He decided, somewhat impulsively, to buy a fifty-acre farm near Ridgefield, Connecticut, and there build a house to his own liking.

That the scheme he had in mind may have been beyond the scope of his immediate resources was nothing new to him—he would have to work that much harder and turn out enough paintings to meet the situation, that was all. He expected to sell the New Rochelle house quite easily, and the stock market was a fine quick way to get hold of the necessary money.

Unluckily, the New Rochelle estate failed to find a buyer for a considerable length of time; instead he was forced to part with his beloved Ingleneuk Island. As for the stock market, a notation in his diary emphasized that he "would rather put his money in manure"; and indeed even before the Ridgefield buildings were completed he found it necessary to sell the "farm," for $40,000, retaining about ten acres surrounding the house and the other buildings he was planning.

The house was large and of his own design. There was a studio so spacious that it would accommodate "a trooper on horseback," and a fine barn for his horses. He had sold the pair of horses he owned, expecting to get at least one fine Arabian from a choice group that his friend Homer Davenport was importing, but in this he was disappointed. Only little "Pinto Pony" remained, who would be the diminutive master in the big stable until more appropriate occupants could be found. He built a special room for storing grain; and a building for chickens. There was also a house for Tim, his man, of whom he was very fond and who was one of his favorite conversationalists. To this imposing group of buildings, friends and neighbors soon began to attach the name "Remington Village," though Remington himself called it "The One Hoss Farm."

Remington supervised all the building, landscaping and other details, going indefatigably back and forth between New Rochelle and Ridgefield, a rather formidable trip in those days. At the same time he was working harder than ever, both on painting and sculpture. But eventually the Ridgefield place was ready to live in.

Moving an establishment such as Remington had gathered together was like moving a Wild West museum, an art gallery and a library, not to mention the usual family furnishings and paraphernalia. He packed everything in his studio himself, and on May 17, 1909, the Remingtons' home was transferred from New Rochelle to Ridgefield.

Ten days later, Emma Caten came to visit them. She had just returned from Europe where she had visited a number of the finest art museums. Anxiously she had looked forward to seeing Frederic's latest work and the progress which she was confident he had been making during her absence. Her admiration of her brother-in-law's work was staunch and sincere, and to her he perhaps talked more openly about his ambitions and despairs than to any other person. He showed her the paintings he had recently finished and those he was still working on, confessing that he believed he was at last making real progress. There had been times, he told her, when he had felt he should somehow have managed to study in Paris or some other place where he would have been under the tutelage of recognized masters. But now, he said, he was thankful there had been no foreign influence to affect his own individual way of working.

Remington was very happy that summer of 1909, and he worked very hard. The pictures that he painted are undoubtedly among the finest of his entire career—"The Outlier," "The Love Call," "Among the Led Horses," "The Buffalo Runners—Big Horn Basin" and others. And he modelled what most critics consider his finest sculpture, "The Stampede"—and was making enthusiastic plans for the future.

He had a great desire to see American public buildings decorated with purely American subjects by American artists, and in this he was considerably in advance of his time. He particularly hoped to do a mural for the Capitol in Albany, picturing the Seneca Indians who were members of its first Assembly. An even more ambitious dream was to model the statue of an American Indian, to be cast in heroic size and placed on Staten Island where it extended farthest into the ocean; a monument to the first inhabitants which would be the first welcome sight of our land from far out at sea.

His exhibition of twenty-three paintings held at Knoedler's galleries in New York City early in December that year was the most successful he had yet held. The critics were especially kind and the sales were good. One review had this to say:

"It must be extremely trying for those commentators on pictorial art who always insisted this distinguished artist was 'only an illustrator,' and decried his ability to paint, to visit such an exhibition as the present one. For by this time, they must be impressed with the fact that Remington's work is splendid in its technique, epic in its

120

imaginative qualities, and historically important in its prominent contributions to the records of the most romantic epoch in the making of the West. American history, so far as it is concerned with the conquest of the plains and the Indians, will be made more vivid to the youths of the future through Remington's canvases and drawings, than through printed pages, no matter who the author."

Another reviewer reported: "Among the large canvases are several which are entitled to rank among the best things which Remington has done. 'The Love Call,' an Indian wooer blowing his flute at the foot of a tree in the enchanted moonlight, is a triumph of a beautiful characterization. Another masterpiece of expression is 'The Luckless Hunter,' an Indian on horseback, moving forlornly homeward through the weird night light. In all of Remington's pictures, the shadow of death seems not far away. If the actors in the vivid scenes are not threatened by death in terrible combat, they are menaced in the form of famine, thirst or cold. One sees the death's head through the skin of the lean faces of his Indians, cowboys and soldiers. . . . The presence, in Mr. Remington's characteristic work, of a great central motive like this . . . is an indication of power, and the ability to express the motive in a hundred vivid forms, is a proof of genius."

And then, three weeks after the exhibition had opened, he was, as he expressed it in his diary for December twentieth, "caught with intense pains in the belly . . . and went to bed so stiff and sore, I could hardly move—and stayed there."

The next day he felt better and did some work. Emma Caten arrived for the holidays. The last words he wrote in his diary were, "Doctor Cook has blown up entirely." The remaining entries, from which this account is drawn, are in his wife's handwriting.

On December twenty-second, they started for town in the morning on the 8:26 train, but the jar of the wagon made Frederic very ill and it seemed that they must turn back. However, he insisted on going on. When they reached the city he admitted to being worse and decided to come back on the noon train, after picking up a painting at the Lincoln National Bank. When they reached home, about three o'clock, he went immediately to bed and Eva sent for Doctor Lowe. The night was spent restlessly and in pain.

On the following day, there were several consultations, with the dread word "cancer" mentioned. Finally it was decided that an emergency operation for appendicitis was called for. Three doctors and two nurses were in attendance, and when he was told they must operate, Frederic's characteristic response was "Cut her loose, Doc."

The operation seemed successful. He was more comfortable and very cheerful, though restless throughout the next night.

Christmas Day broke stormily, with high winds and heavy snow. The family opened packages in the morning, and for a few hours it seemed as though it might be a happy Christmas after all. But early in the afternoon his condition changed. The doctors told Eva frankly that it was the beginning of the end; his system was so poisoned that he could not throw it off. "He was cheerful and felt he was better," she wrote. "It was probably the lack of pain that made him so."

The storm continued violently through the night; the winds were still high and the roads badly drifted. But in the morning the snow had stopped falling—the storm had subsided. At half-past nine Frederic Remington drew his last breath.

Thus, so shortly after passing his forty-eighth birthday, and so soon after coming to the goal which he had striven so hard to reach, Frederic Remington suddenly came to the end of the trail.

Only a small group of close friends attended the quiet funeral services held on December twenty-seventh in the Ridgefield home: Emma Caten, E. W. Kemble, Augustus Thomas, Childe Hassam, Riccardo Bertelli, Irving Bacheller, A. Barton Hepburn, and a few others. Then Eva took him back to Canton and he was buried there next day in Evergreen Cemetery. A plain gravestone bears the one word REMINGTON, and a small headstone carries his name and date of birth and death. His own chosen epitaph, "He Knew the Horse," is written large throughout his work—and to this can appropriately be added, "He knew the Cowboy, and the Indian, and all else that went to make up the Old West," as no other artist has ever known them.

Bibliographic Check List
of Remingtoniana

Although Frederic Remington died at the comparatively early age of forty-eight, after only twenty-three years of active work in his profession, he completed a total of at least 2,739 drawings and paintings which have been reproduced for public benefit. These pictures have appeared in forty-one different periodicals and 142 books. Some of the periodicals used hundreds of Remington's pictures. Many of the pictures have been repeatedly reprinted, both in magazines and books. Many of them have also been made into art plates for distribution individually, or in portfolios, as calendars, posters, or included in collected works of art. Eight of the books were written by Remington himself; and many of the others have been re-published in several formats and in foreign editions. In addition, Remington did twenty-five works of sculpture that were cast in bronze; and he wrote scores of articles and stories.

The following is intended primarily as a complete record of Frederic Remington's pictures and the publications in which they have appeared. The tabulations have been arranged under the following classifications: Periodicals, listed alphabetically according to name of publication. Books, written and illustrated by Remington, in chronological order. Books and portfolios of pictures by Remington, chronologically arranged. Books illustrated entirely or in part by this artist, or containing his pictures, alphabetically arranged according to authors. Books containing references to Remington or his work, alphabetically by authors. And a list of his bronzes, with descriptions.

The first appearance of each of the 2,739 Frederic Remington pictures is established in these lists. In all cases where the title and page number are given, this indicates a first appearance, unless otherwise stated.

The bibliographic data on the first editions of books have been compiled with the assistance of E. Walter Latendorf, and the periodical lists with the assistance of H. Conrad McCracken, to whom this writer is deeply indebted. The measurements given are for outside covers.

Most of the information compiled in this bibliographic check list is drawn from the private collection of this biographer.

KEY TO ABBREVIATIONS

p. (page, *pl.* pp.)

f-p. (full-page)

d-p. (double-page)

f-c. (full-color)

illus. (illustration or illustrations)

front. (frontispiece)

adv. (advertisement)

(   ) indicate description supplied by author

HM (*Harper's Monthly*)

HW (*Harper's Weekly*)

Periodicals

The Interpreter Waved at the Youth
. . ., Semi-color f-p. 131
"I Will Tell the White Man . . .,"
Semi-color f-p. 133
Nothing but Cheerful Looks . . .,
Semi-color f-p. 134

1906

JAN. *The Way of an Indian*, Frederic
Remington, Part V
The Fire Eater Raised His Arms . . .,
front.
He Rushed the Pony . . ., f-p. 311
The Fire Eater Slung His Victim
Across His Pony, f-p. 312
FEB. *The Way of an Indian*, Frederic
Remington, Part VII
(Indian Chief on charging horse)
f-c. cover
The Rushing Red Lodges Passed
Through the Line . . ., (same as
cover, in black-and-white), f-p.
379
MARCH *The Way of an Indian*, Frederic
Remington, Part VIII
He Made His Magazine Gun Blaze
Until Empty, f-p. 564
He Shouted His Harsh Pathos . . .,
f-p. 567

CRAFTSMAN

1909

MARCH *Frederic Remington—Painter
and Sculptor: A Pioneer in Dis-
tinctive American Art*, Giles Ed-
gerton
10 illus. by Remington from *Collier's*

CURRENT LITERATURE

1907

Nov. *Frederic Remington—A Painter
of the Vanishing West*
5 Remington illus. from *Collier's*
and portrait.

EVERYBODY'S

1901

SEPT. *Billy the Kid*, E. Hough
"He Was the Law," f-p. 303

1902

FEB. *A Lasso Duel*, William Bulfin
"It was to be a Lasso Duel . . .,"
front.
MAY *The Baptism of the Buzzards*,
Frederick Walworth
"The Lawyer-Colonel Did It . . .,"
f-p. 472
Nov. *The Round Table of Dodge City,*
E. C. Little

"The Only Descendant of Cotton
Mather . . .," f-p. 436

1903

AUG. *Don Goyo's Holy Remedy*, Wil-
liam Bulfin
(Horsemen on Mexican street) p.
171
Candido Ramos, the Wolf of the
West, p. 172

1905

JAN. *La Quemazon*, William Bulfin
"I Could Hear the Gathering Thun-
der of Their Hoofs . . .," f-p. 89

GRIDIRON, THE

1882

—— Beta Zeta Chapter of Beta Theta
Pi Fraternity, St. Lawrence Univ.
(pamphlet)
A Class in Surveying [Page of
sketches]

HARPER'S BAZAR

1887

MAY 21 Glove Making in Fulton
County [9 sketches], f-p. 369

1893

DEC. 16 *The Vow of the Virgin's
Heart*, M. G. McClelland
"I Whistled and Sang . . ."; "He Lay
Where He had Been Jerked . . .,"
p. 1028

1899

JULY 1 "In Fishing Time."

HARPER'S MONTHLY
MAGAZINE

1889

Nov. *The Mexican Army*, Thomas A.
Janvier
A Regimental Scout, front.
Artillery Sergeant, p. 813
Undress Engineer, p. 814
Full-Dress Engineer, p. 815
Type of Officer: "Awfully French,"
p. 816
Drum Corps, f-p. 817
Looking for Deserters, p. 818
Lieutenant, Engineer Battalion, p.
819
Bugler of Cavalry, f-p. 821
A Gendarme, p. 822
Infantry of the Line, f-p. 823
A Rural, p. 824
Cavalry of the Line, f-p. 825

Stable Call at an Artillery Barrack,
p. 826

1890

JULY *Texan Types and Contrasts*, Lee
C. Harby
An Olla; A Mexican Vendor, p. 229
Woman Vending Fruit on a Street
Corner, p. 230
A Mexican Two-wheeled cart, p. 231
Mexican Jacals, p. 232
Mexican Vendor and Child, p. 233
A Greaser, or the Lower Type of
Mexican, p. 234
The Tortilla-Maker, p. 235
Woman Grinding on the Metal, p.
236
Juan and Juanita, p. 237
A Mexican Vaquero, p. 238
Riding the Line of the Wire Fence,
p. 239
A Noonday Siesta in the Street, p.
240
A Mexican Buccaro, p. 241
The Water-cart, p. 243
The Banjo Player, p. 244
Mexican Woman Washing, p. 245
SEPT. *Across the Andes*, Theodore Child
Roping Cattle at Punta Negra, p. 491
OCT. *Antoine's Moose-Yard*, Julian
Ralph
A Moose Bull Fight, front.
(Initial sketch of Remington &
Ralph) p. 651
The Hotel: Last Sign of Civilization,
p. 653
"Give Me a Light," p. 655
Antoine, From Life, p. 656
The Portage Sleigh on a Lumber
Road, p. 657
"The Track in the Winter Forest,"
f-p. 659
Pierre, From Life, p. 660
Antoine's Cabin, p. 661
The Camp at Night, p. 662
On the Moose Trail, p. 663
In Sight of the Game . . ., f-p. 665
Success, p. 666
OCT. *Agricultural Chili*, Theodore
Child
A Vaquero, f-p. 771
Ox Cart, Traiguen, p. 782
Nov. *Our Italy*, Charles Dudley Warner
(Sketch of Indian woman) p. 814
(2 sketches of Indian men) p. 815

1891

MARCH *The Chinese Leak*, Julian
Ralph
(Sketch of Chinaman with baskets)
p. 517

a Scholar, But He Didn't Look the Part," p. 267

"Stop—Stop That, Dan!" f-p. 268

APRIL *They Bore a Hand*, Frederic Remington

"Get Down," p. 705

"There Was Nothing to Do," f-p. 707

"I Hope the Colonel Won't Get Mad——", p. 709

The Death of Oestreicher, p. 711

MAY *The Game and the Nation*, Owen Wister

"Poker? With Them Kittens?", p. 887

"Have Your Bottle, Then," p. 890

" 'Afraid?' He Sneered," p. 894

The Frog-Story, f-p. 903

1901

FEB. *Natchez's Pass*, Frederic Remington

The Captain . . . Looked at the Moon, p. 441

Pushed Himself Back in His Chair Before the Horrible Sight, f-p. 442

MARCH *The Soft-Hearted Sioux*, Zit-kala-Sa

At My Feet a Man's Figure Lay, f-p. 509

APRIL *Colonies and Nation*, Woodrow Wilson

At the Iroquois Council Fire, f-p. 723

JUNE *Colonies and Nation*, Woodrow Wilson

The Morning of the Battle of the Plains of Abraham, f-p. 129

1902

DEC. (Adv.) "With the Wolf Hounds"

HARPER'S ROUND TABLE

1896

APRIL 7 *How to Start in Life*, Hon. Theodore Roosevelt

2 Remington illus. from *H.M.*

AUG. 4 *Held Captive by Savages*, Capt. Howard Patterson

1 Remington illus. from *H.M.*

1897

FEB. 16 *Bear Hunting*, Caspar Whitney

1 Remington illus. from *H.M.*

APRIL 27 *In the Transvaal of Today*, V. Gribayedoff

2 Remington illus. from *H.M.*

MAY 4 *The Soledad Girls*, Fred Remington

The Half Wild Cattle Came Down from the Hills, cover, p. 641

MAY 25 *Marshal Castellane's Aids*, George B. Mallon

1 Remington illus. from *H.M.*

1898

APRIL *The Game Warden's Story*, Frank L. Pollock

1 Remington illus. from *H.M.*

HARPER'S WEEKLY

1882

FEB. 25 Cow-boys of Arizona: Roused by a Scout. Drawn by W. A. Rogers from a Sketch by Frederic Remington. f-p. 120

1885

MARCH 28 Ejecting an "Oklahoma Boomer." Drawn by T. de Thulstrup from a Sketch by Frederic Remington. Front cover, p. 193

1886

JAN. 9 The Apache War: Indian Scouts on Geronimo's Trail, front.

JAN. 30 "The Apaches are Coming," f-p. 76

APRIL 24 "The Fourth Trooper," p. 268

MAY 29 "Shot on Picket." Drawn by T. de Thulstrup from a sketch by Frederic Remington. D-p. 344-45

JULY 17 Signalling the Main Command, p. 452

AUG. 7 Mexican Troops in Sonora [5 sketches], f-p. 509

AUG. 21 Soldiering in the Southwest: The Rescue of Corporal Scott, front., p. 529

Types From Arizona [13 sketches], p. 532

Our Soldiers in the Southwest, p. 535

SEPT. 4 "Abandoned," front., p. 561

"Saddle Up," p. 567

SEPT. 25 The Apache Campaign: Burial of Hatfield's Men, p. 617

OCT. 9 In From the Night Herd, front., p. 645

The Couriers, p. 655

1887

JAN. 15 Pima Indians Convoying a Silver Train in Mexico, f-p. 37

FEB. 19 Sketches on a Man-of-War Under Sailing Orders, f-p. 137

APRIL 2 Sketches Among the Papagos [12 sketches], f-p. 244

APRIL 23 A Quarrel Over Cards, f-p. 301

MAY 7 Buffalo Dance, f-p. 332

JUNE 18 A False Start, p. 436

A Close Finish, p. 436

JULY 23 In the Lodges of the Blackfeet Indians [9 sketches], f-p. 521

SEPT. 17 Burning the Range, front., p. 661

OCT. 1 Training U. S. Troops in Indian Warfare [8 sketches], f-p. 713

NOV. 5 Crow Indians Firing into Agency, f-p. 800

NOV. 26 College Players at Football, front., p. 849

DEC. 24 Canadian Mounted Police on a "Musical Ride," f-p. 945

1888

FEB. 4 Arrest of a Blackfoot Murderer [Sketch], p. 80

MARCH 31 Arrest of a Blackfoot Murderer, p. 233

APRIL 28 Texan Cattle in a Kansas Corn Corral, p. 300

MAY 5 Yaqui Indian Refugees with Captive Mexican Soldier, f-p. 316

MAY 26 An Ox Train in the Mountains, p. 380

AUG. 4 *Skirmish Drill of the N. Y. National Guard*

"Rally on the Battalion," p. 572-73

"Fire Kneeling—Aim!"; "Commence Firing!"; "Oh! My Shoulder!"; A Cartridge Stuck; "Don't Understand the Call"; "Advance Loading," p. 572

A Line Officer, p. 572-73

A File Closer; "Cease Firing"; In the Woods; The Bugler; "In Place, Rest!"; "Double Time!"; "Load!" p. 573

AUG. 18 Geronimo and His Band Returning From Raid into Mexico, f-p. 609

AUG. 25 A Fur Train from the Far North, p. 636

SEPT. 15 Water Jump at Cederhurst, f-p. 693

OCT. 6 Her First Muskallonge, front., p. 745

OCT. 6 *Sketches from the Fleetwood Trotting Track*

Warming: a Study of Action, p. 749

Explaining Defeat to the Owners, p. 749

A Break, p. 749

"You Suah Lose Dat Two Dollars Jim," p. 749

Ready for a Heat, p. 749

Interested Parties, p. 758

OCT. 13 Sketches of the Canadian Mounted Police [13 sketches], f-p. 780

OCT. 27 Dragging a Bull's Hide Over a Prairie Fire, d-p. 826-27

Battery K at Drill in the Berkshire Hills, f-p. 770

Captain Dillenback [sketch]; Stable Frock; The First Sergeant, Battery K, 1st Artillery, in Field Trim, p. 771

Nov. 16 Getting Hunters in Horse-Show Form, f-p. 1087

Dec. 14 *A Journey in Search of Christmas*, Owen Wister

"Ah, You Come Along with Us: We'll Take Yer!" p. 1182

" 'Changed My Mind,' said Lin, Grinning," p. 1184

1896

Jan. 4 A Practice March in Texas, f-p. 16

Jan. 25 Paying the Indians for the Cherokee Strip, f-p. 81

March 7 The Flag of Cuba—Insurgent Cavalry Drawn Up for a Charge, cover, p. 217

March 28 *Squadron A's Games*, Frederic Remington

Over the Hurdle with a Cut at the Leather Head; Picking Up the Handkerchief; Tent - Pegging; Mannikin Race, p. 293

April 4 Miners Boating Down the Yukon River, Alaska, p. 316

Miners with Their Supplies Crossing Lake Lindemann, p. 316

May 2 *A New Idea for Soldiers*, Frederic Remington

The Yoke [sketch]; Side View; The Dodge Field Equipment . . ., p. 442

May 16 Spring Fishing in Canada: A Good Day's Sport, f-p. 501

May 23 England's Fighting Force in Egypt . . ., f-p. 512

June 27 Slatin Pasha and His Performing Horse, Plum Pudding, p. 635

Aug. 8 Hasty Entrenchment Drill . . ., f-p. 773

Aug. 29 Uprising of the Yaqui Indians: Yaqui Warriors in Retreat, p. 857

Oct. 3 Moose Hunting: An Unexpected Shot, f-p. 976

His Bag, p. 984

Nov. 14 A Loser at the Horse Show; A Winner, p. 1122

Nov. 28 "White Man's Big Sunday" . . ., f-p. 1168

Dec. 12 Leadville's Determined Strike . . ., front., p. 1209

1897

Jan. 9 A Tug-of-War on Field Sport Day: Infantry *vs.* Cavalry, p. 41

Jan. 30 Winter Pastimes at an Army Post in the Southwest . . ., f-p. 109

June 26 Tarpon Fishing in Florida: The Jump, p. 640

Oct. 2 A Wounded Bull Elk, cover, p. 965

Nov. 20 Going to the Horse Show, p. 1149

1898

Jan. 29 *A Winter Trip Through Yellowstone Park*, Lieut. Elmer Lindsay

"Beaver Dick"; Wading an Icy Stream, p. 106

Cavalry Officers Inspecting Yellowstone Park in Winter, p. 107

U. S. Cavalryman at one of the Soldier Stations in Yellowstone Park, p. 110

March 26 A First Lesson in the Art of War, cover, p. 289

April 2 Maj. Gen. Nelson A. Miles, U.S.A. Inspecting the Defenses of New York, f-p. 320

April 2 *The Training of Cavalry*, Frederic Remington

Hurdling on Three Horses, p. 321

A Roman Race at the Riding Hall, Fort Meyer, Virginia, d-p. 324-25

May 14 *Wigwags From the Blockade*, Frederic Remington

(Sketch of naval officer), p. 462

Watching the Big Search-lights in Havana; Wigwagging With a Dark Lantern, p. 464

May 21 With the Regulars at Port Tampa, Florida: 9th U. S. Cavalry Skirmishing Through the Pines, d-p. 492-93

May 28 Colored Troopers of 9th U. S. Cavalry Taking Their Horses for a Dash into the Gulf, f-p. 508

Lieut.-Col. Wallace F. Randolph, U.S.A., p. 509

C. E. Akers, Correspondent of London "Times"; Capt. Arthur H. Lee, R.A., at Tampa; Richard Harding Davis, at Tampa, p. 510

The "Gussie" Expedition: First Embarkation of U. S. Troops for Cuba, at Port Tampa, May 11, p. 525

June 4 *Some Notable General Officers at Tampa, Florida*

Maj.-Gen. William R. Shafter, U. S. Vols.; Maj.-Gen. James F. Wade, U. S. Vols.; Brig.-Gen. Guy V. Henry, U. S. Vols.; Maj.-Gen. Joseph Wheeler, U. S. Vols., p. 536

June 11 *Prominent Officers Now at Tampa, Florida*

Lieut. Count A. v. Goetzen (Ger-

many); Brig.-Gen. Samuel S. Sumner, U. S. Vols.; Brig.-Gen. Adna R. Chaffee, U. S. Vols.; Brig.-Gen. William Ludlow, U. S. Vols., p. 566

June 18 U. S. Cavalry Passing Army Pack-Train on the Road, d-p. 592-93

Aug. 6 The Storming of San Juan, July 1, d-p. 768-69

Oct. 1 Captain Allyn Capron, U.S.A., p. 973

Dec. 24 Field Hospital at the "Bloody Ford" on San Juan Creek, d-p. 1268-69

1899

May 13 The Philippines: Brig.-Gen. Lloyd Wheaton, U.S.V., Ordering the Advance at Stone Quarry Hill, cover, p. 467

May 20 The Rainy Season in the Philippines . . ., p. 502

May 27 The Philippines: American Soldiers Swimming to an Assault on the Insurgent Entrenchments, f-p. 526

June 3 Maj.-Gen. Henry W. Lawton, U.S.V., cover, p. 539

June 10 In the Philippines: A Bayonet Rush, d-p. 574-75

July 15 How the Horses Died for Their Country at Santiago, d-p. 698-99

Oct. 14 Boer Scouts on the Natal Border, cover, p. 1033

Boers in Camp, p. 1036

Nov. 18 Schooling Hunters for the Horse-Show, f-p. 1061

Dec. 16 *The Military Search for Belle McKeever, Fitz-James McCarthy*

(Belle McKeever and soldier on horses), f-c. p. 17

"We are Doomed" (color); The Old Water-Scout (color); Desert Canteens (color), p. 18

"In Half an Hour He Was Senseless: By Three o'Clock He Was Dead" (color); Old Fort Yuma (color), p. 23

"He Seemed to Have Fallen Into a Gloomy Dementia . . ." (color), f-p. 24

1900

Feb. 10 The War in South Africa: A Close Call for Remington's Scouts, f-p. 123

March 10 The Frozen Sheep-Herder, d-p. 224-25

March 24 Working Snow-Bound Ponies Out of the Mountains, f-p. 276

Oct. 27 The 9th U. S. Infantry Entering Peking, d-p. 1012-13
Nov. 3 The Drought in the Southwest, d-p. 1038-39

1901

March 2 On Ore Train Going Into the Silver-Mines, Colorado, d-p. 226-27

HARPER'S YOUNG PEOPLE

1887

Feb. 8 *A Hunt for Young Antelope*, F. Schwatka

1894

Nov. 20 *Early Days of Successful Men*, Capt. C. A. Curtis
1 Remington illus. from *Harper's*

HOUND & HORN

1933

July-Sept. *Remington and Winslow Homer*, John Wheelwright
3 Remington illus. from *Harper's*

HOUSTON, MUSEUM OF FINE ARTS OF—BULLETIN

1944

Spring The Remington Collection, catalogue and 1 Remington illus.

INTERNATIONAL STUDIO

1923

Feb. *Remington at Twenty-three*, Mrs. Nellie Hough
5 Remington illus. from pictures made in Kansas City *c.* 1884:
  "Gracias Senora! May the Apaches Never Get You"; "Old Dick," p. 13
  "Sentinels on Guard"; "The Cattle Rustlers," p. 14
  "The Prairie Fire," p. 15

LIFE

1903

Feb. 5 (Adv.) "The Last Stand"

1942

Sept. 24 *Frederic Remington*
Portrait, photos of 6 Bronzes and 8 f-c. illus.

LONDON GRAPHIC

1887

March 26 Uncle Sam's Last Fight [8 Sketches]

1889

March 30 A Trooper of the Canadian Mounted Police Lost
June 28 Arrest of a Half-Breed Whiskey Smuggler

McCLURE'S MAGAZINE

1899

June *With Troop M on the Frontier*, W. J. Carney
  ". . . the Thermometer From Ten to Thirty Degrees Below Zero . . .," f-p. 126
  "We Discovered . . . Three Men Lying Dead . . .," f-p. 128

1900

Nov. *Confusion of Goods*, Frederic C. Baldy
  "Wright Had a Circular Course . . .," p. 13
  "When the Players Were Pulled Off . . .," p. 14

1901

March *Billy's Tearless Woe*, Frederic Remington
  (Man and dog in front of tent), p. 455
  "Billy, I Find Him Dog . . .," p. 457
  The Burial of Keno, p. 458

MENTOR

1915

June 15 *Painters of Western Life*, Arthur Hoeber
  The Last Stand, f-p., insert intagliogravure

METROPOLITAN

1896

July *Artist Remington at Home and Afield*, C. M. Fairbanks
  5 photos and 6 illus. by Remington, incl. 3 originals:
  Study of a Cow Pony, p. 446
  Guard House, Camp Eagle Pass, Texas, p. 448
  The Herd, p. 450

1906

May (Adv.) "Arizona Cowboy" (verso Table of Contents)
June *A Bunch of Buckskins*, Owen Wister
  "A Regular," p. 287
  "Cavalry Officer," p. 288
  "An Old-Time Trapper," p. 289

  "An Arizona Cowboy," f-p. 290
  "A North-west Half-Breed," f-p. 291
  "Old Ramon, a Mexican Half-Breed," f-p. 292
  "A War Chief," f-p. 293
  "A Black-foot Brave," p. 294

1908

Jan. *The Border Breed*, B. Briscoe
  "A Cavalryman Alert, Was a Rest for Nerves," p. 485

NEWSWEEK

1946

July 8 *Remington's New Frontier*
1 Remington illus., p. 88

NEW YORK JOURNAL (Newspaper)

1897

Jan. 24 Spanish Guerillas Bringing "Pacificos" Into Camp, f-p.
  A Spanish Soldier; A Spanish Officer, f-p.
Jan. 29 A Familiar Incident of the Cuban War, f-p.
Jan. 31 *Richard Harding Davis, War Correspondent*
  (Caption same as title. Portrays Davis on horseback, in typical Remington fashion, but head and face redrawn by another, more glamorizing artist)
  Amateur Surgery in Cuba; Bringing in the Wounded; A Spanish Guerrilla
Feb. 2 Moonlight Execution of Young Rodriguez
Feb. 12 Spaniards Search Women on American Steamer
Feb. 28 Spanish Cavalryman on a Texas Bronco

1898

April 26 The Advance Guard of the Army
April 27 Soldiers in Woolen Clothing
May 8 Yankee Guns in the Orient and the Noble Avenge of the Maine: 24 heads of U. S. sailors
  Group of U. S. sailors
May 11 The Army Pack Mule Ready to Assail the Spaniards; An Army Train All Ready for the Invasion
May 14 American Soldier, Fit for Fighting; The Man Who Gives the Command
May 17 Ninth Cavalry, Colored Troops, on Washing Duty; U. S. Troops Practicing Marching in Palmettos; The Orderly Trumpeter

APRIL-MAY-JUNE 1 f-p. illus. by Remington from *H. M.*

1894

JAN.-FEB.-MARCH Sketch "Study of Legs," p. 79
"An Old Friend," p. 83
JULY-AUG.-SEPT. An Old Favorite, p. 311
OCT.-NOV.-DEC. Bronco, p. 436

ST. NICHOLAS

1886

NOV. *Juan and Juanita*, Frances C. Baylor
A Mexican Hacienda, p. 34
"Don Jose's Vicious Little Mustang Bolted . . .," p. 37

1888

MARCH *Tom's Ride*, Robert E. Tener
"Tom Kicked Away the Stirrups . . .," p. 358
SEPT. *Some Stories About "The California Lion,"* E. P. Roe
"Spurring His Horse in Pursuit . . .," p. 815
The Mare Defends Her Colt, p. 816

1889

NOV. *A Story of a Horse*, Capt. C. A. Curtis
"Will the Liftinent Plaze to Come Out . . .," p. 33
"Two-Bits' Last Dash," p. 35
DEC. *Buffalo Hunting*, Theodore Roosevelt
"They Were in Good Training . . .," p. 140
A Thrilling Experience of Life on the Plains . . ., p. 141
Taking Hides After a Hunt, p. 142
"The Great Beast Came Crashing to the Earth," p. 142
A War Party of Comanches "Jumping" a Hunter's Camp; (Tailpiece of coyote and buffalo skull), p. 143

1890

DEC. *A Race with Idaho Robbers*, Joaquin Miller
(Rough-appearing white man on a horse), p. 138
"My Pursuers Were Not a Hundred Yards Behind Me," f-p. 141

1910

APRIL *Books, Reading*
1 Remington illus. from *The Century*

1923

APRIL *From Express in a Satchel to*

Routes Through the Air, Boardman Pickett
2 Remington illus. from *The Century*

SATURDAY EVENING POST, THE

1901

OCT. 26 *Superstition Trail*, Owen Wister, Part I
"You're Hanging Them Tomorrow," f-p. 3
NOV. 2 *Superstition Trail*, Owen Wister, Part II
"Then He Very Slowly Turned Round . . .," p. 7
DEC. 4 (Indian on horseback). Cover in red-and-black

1903

FEB. 7 (Adv.) "The Last Stand," p. 19

1922

JAN. 14 *The Print of My Remembrance*, Augustus Thomas
Pen-and-Ink Sketch of F. W. Ruckstull; of William Marion Reedy, p. 12

SCRIBNER'S MAGAZINE

1889

JULY *How the Derby Was Won*, Harrison Robertson
(Initial sketch of colored jockey), p. 24
"A Good Half Hour Was Then Wasted . . .," f-p. 37
"Winner, By a Head, of the Kentucky Derby," p. 38
"Put Me Down, Quick, Quick," p. 39
"Yaboo," p. 40

1892

MARCH *American Illustration of To-day*, William A. Coffin
"The Bookmaker," p. 340

1893

OCT. *The Northwest Mounted Police of Canada*, J. G. A. Creighton
(Initial sketch of Canadian policeman), p. 399
Officer of the Mounted Police in Full-dress, f-p. 401
Police Recruit Acquiring a Military Seat, p. 402
Street Dress of the Mounted Police, p. 403
A Serious Warning, f-p. 405
Police and Trailer Following a Criminal, p. 408
Winter Costume of the Police, p. 409

One of the Riders, p. 411
Daring Arrest of Bull Elk . . ., f-p. 412

1899

APRIL *The Rough Riders*, Theodore Roosevelt
Charge of the Rough Riders at San Juan Hill, f-p. 421

1901

NOV. *The United States Army*, Francis V. Greene
The Defeat of "Crazy Horse" by Col. Mills, January 1877, f-p. 595

1902

AUG. (Adv.) "Hands Off," p. 57
OCT. *Western Types*, Frederic Remington
The Cowboy, f-c. f-p. 409
The Cossack Post (Cavalryman), f-c. f-p. 411
The Scout, f-c. f-p. 413
The Half-Breed, f-c. f-p. 415

1910

FEB. *Frederic Remington: A Painter of American Life*, Royal Cortissoz
The Luckless Hunter, p. 181
The Winter Campaign, f-p. 183
The Gossips, f-p. 185
The War Bridle, p. 186
The Hunters' Supper, p. 187
The Love Call, p. 188
The Outlier, p. 189
The Moose Country, p. 190
Among the Led Horses, f-p. 191
The Buffalo Runners: Big Horn Basin, f-p. 193
The White Country, p. 194

1937

JAN. Fiftieth Anniversary Number
1 Remington illus., "The Cowboy," f-c.

SUCCESS

1899

MAY 13 *Remington and His Work*, Charles H. Garrett
1 Remington illus. from *Drawings*, 1 portrait and 2 photos

TELEGRAPH (SUNDAY)

1903

NOV. 8 Scene from *John Ermine of the Yellowstone* at the Manhattan Theatre (N. Y.)

TIME

1946

JULY 15 *He Knew the Horse*
2 Remington illus. The picture "The Captive," which is attributed to Remington, is not authentic

WOMAN'S HOME COMPANION

1903

JUNE Custer's Last Fight, p. 31

WORLD'S WORK

1905

AUG. "The Lewis and Clark Fair," Robertus Love
Photo of heroic group "Hitting the Trail" ["Coming Through the Rye"]
(Adv.) 3 illus. from *Collier's*

YALE COURANT

1879

Nov. 2 "College Riff-Raff," IV, p. 47
(Remington's first published picture)

YOUTH'S COMPANION, THE

1888

FEB. 2 Tracing a Watch, p. 50
FEB. 23 *The Cowboy's Verdict*, R. G. Carter
(Head of Indian); (Trooper and Indian on horses); (A Frontier Jury), p. 94

MARCH 1 *One Touch of Nature*, L. D. Leech
(Frontiersman on horseback); (Cowboy with saddle); (A lynching party), p. 99
MARCH 1 *Ojibbwa Magic*, Dr. G. Archie Stockwell
"Medicine Elk," p. 101
MARCH 15 *Trapped by "Traveling Mountain,"* Frank W. Calkins
Digging Us Out, p. 127
MARCH 22 *Waneepah*, F. Janvrin
Waneepah, p. 145
MAY 24 *Hostin Kar*, John Willis Hayes
Hostin Kar Uses a Telescope, p. 255
MAY 31 *On the Texas Cow-Trail*, B. G. A.
(Nigger Joe); (Driving cattle through town); (Driving cattle), p. 267
JUNE 21 *Old Jimmy's Story*, G. A. Leigh
(Old Jim telling a story); (Saddling a pony), p. 303
JUNE 28 *Marcellino and Tecalotina*, Clarence Pullen
(Indians capturing a boy), p. 314
(Boy on donkey), p. 315
JULY 19 *The Pawkeet Marauder*, E. L. Chichester
(A mountain lion), p. 351
JULY 26 *Maquina's Mantle*, Robert Kelson
(Indian woman delivering a note); (Maquina displaying the mantle), p. 363

SEPT. 27 *Sequapah*, Frank W. Calkins
Unwelcome Visitors, p. 459
OCT. 11 *"Khe-be-ashtie,"* John Willis Hayes
(Negro trooper and Indians); (Khe-be-ashtie), p. 483
OCT. 18 *Clyde's Adventure*, G. A. Leigh
(Indian being thrown from horse), p. 501
(Cowboy galloping away from Indians), p. 502
Nov. 15 *The Cowboy's Duel*, H. P. Ufford
(Cowboy riding a steer), p. 582

1889

MARCH 14 *Jeff the "Horse Wrangler,"* F. S. Davis
(A running fight with horse thieves), p. 138
APRIL 25 *Francisco*, John Willis Hayes
Hamlin and the Navajos, p. 219
Arresting Cattle-Thieves, p. 226
MAY 2 *Brimstone*, Clarence Pullen
An Astonished Mule, p. 231
MAY 9 *A Vacation Tour*, M. M. Ballou
Following the Trail, p. 249
MAY 23 *Policemen of the Canadian Plains*, J. M. Oxley
A Mounted Policeman, p. 273
AUG. 1 *A Military Tournament*, Wm. H. Rideling
(Caption same as title), p. 388
DEC. 19 *Attacked by Cheyennes*, K. L. O. F. Wolcott
"You'll Have to Get Out of This," p. 672

Books Written and Illustrated by Frederic Remington

Pony Tracks, Harper & Brothers, N. Y., Copyright April 3, 1895. ¶ Gilt lettering and pictorial Indian design on dark buckskin-colored cloth. 8vo. 6¼" x 9". ¶ Also in full leather. ¶ Remington's first book. A collection of articles and 70 illus. previously published in *H. M.*
A Rogers Ranger in the French and Indian War, Harper & Brothers, N. Y., 1897. ¶ Original printed wrappers. 8vo. 12 pages. ¶ A reprint of "Joshua Goodenough's Old Letter" which appeared in *H. M.*, Nov. 1897. ¶ Scarce.
Crooked Trails, Harper & Brothers, N. Y., Copyright May 26, 1898. ¶ Green lettering and pictorial on buckskin-colored cloth, gilt top; 8vo. 6⅛" x 9". ¶ A collection of articles

and 49 illus. previously published in *H. M.*
——, Harper & Brothers, London and N. Y., 1898. ¶ Gilt lettering on slate-colored cloth. Cover decoration taken from "On The Moose Trail," *H. M.* Oct. 1890, p. 663. 8vo. 6⅜" x 9¼".
——, Foreword by Zane Grey. Harper & Brothers, N. Y., 1923. ¶ Green lettering on straw-colored cloth. 8vo. 6½" x 9⅝".
Sundown Leflare, Harper & Brothers, N. Y. Copyright Jan. 4, 1899. ¶ White lettering and colored pictorial design on wine-colored cloth. 12mo. 5⅛" x 7½". ¶ Five of the "Sundown" stories and 12 illus. previously published in *H. M.*
Stories of Peace and War, Harper & Brothers, N. Y., Copyright Oct. 10,

1899. ¶ Silver lettering and design on slate-blue cloth. 16mo. 3½" x 6⅜". ¶ All copies examined misspell Remington's first name as "Frederick" on cover. ¶ Three articles & 2 illus. previously published in *H. M.*
Men with the Bark On, Harper & Brothers, N. Y., Copyright Jan. 30, 1900. ¶ Red lettering and green design on light-brown cloth. 12mo. 5" x 7½". First Edition of this book issued on both thin and thick paper (approx. ⅞" and 1⅛" across covers) with no priority established. ¶ Collection of articles and 32 illus. previously published in *H. M.*
John Ermine of the Yellowstone, The Macmillan Company, N. Y., Copyright Nov. 12, 1902. ¶ White letter-

ing and portrait design on dark-brown cloth; gilt top. 12mo. 5½″ x 7¾″. ¶ All copies of First Edition examined have author's name misspelled "Reminigton" on spine; corrected in later edition. ¶ Original story and pictures.

John Ermine, Front.; (Initial sketch of miner with pick) p. 1; The Chairman (head), p. 5; (Initial sketch of Indian head), p. 12; A Crow (Indian head), p. 15; "In The Middle of the Bunch Sat Weasel," p. 31; (Initial sketch of horse feeding), p. 37; "He Called the Boy to Him and Put His Arm Around Him," p. 47; Wolf-Voice, p. 84; (Initial of rider and led horse) p. 86; "Halt! Who Goes

There?" p. 97; (Chapter heading of line of heads), p. 101; Captain Lewis (head), p. 105; (Chapter heading of rifle), p. 115; Major Ben Searles (head), p. 117; "Bullets Kicked Up the Dust," p. 127; (Initial of soldier), p. 134; (Initial of river boat), p. 137; Katherine (drawn by Charles Dana Gibson), p. 142; The Englishman (head), p. 144; "Will You Please Carry My Parasol for Me?" (drawn by Charles Dana Gibson), p. 157; Shockley (head), p. 182; (Initial of a magpie), p. 198; "He Bore the Limp Form to the Sands," p. 209; (Initial of man on horse), p. 217; (Initial of man on

horse), p. 229; "A Tremendous Bang Roared Around the Room," p. 239; (Initial of buffalo skull), p. 247; Ramon (head), p. 254

The Way of an Indian, Fox, Duffield & Company, Copyright Feb. 16, 1906. ¶ Yellow lettering and full-color pictorial paper label, on red cloth. 8vo. 5⅞″ x 8⅛″. ¶ First Edition with Fox, Duffield & Company on foot of spine. Earliest state of sheets has p. 9 so numbered. Second Edition with Duffield on foot of spine and without yellow lettering. ¶ Appeared serially in *Cosmopolitan Magazine*. 14 illus. ¶ A Merle Johnson *High Spots of American Literature*.

Books and Portfolios of Pictures by Frederic Remington

Drawings, Foreword by Owen Wister, R. H. Russell, N. Y., 1897. ¶ Black lettering and colored illustration on cream-colored boards, with brown buckram spine. Oblong folio, 11⅞″ x 18⅛″. Boxed. Not paginated. ¶ 62 original pictures:
(Mounted cowboy), color cover
Forsythe's Fight on the Republican River, 1868: The Charge of Roman Nose
Coronado's March: Colorado
The Missionary and the Medicine Man
Hunting a Beaver Stream, 1840
The Hungry Winter
Fight Over a Water Hole
When His Heart Is Bad
A Citadel of the Plains
On the Northwest Coast
The Sheep Herder's Breakfast
The Gold Bug
An Overland Station: Indians Coming in with the Stage
The Well in the Desert
The Borderland of the Other Tribe
Her Calf
A Government Pack Train
The Charge
The Pony War-Dance
The Coming Storm
His Death Song
Protecting a Wagon Train
The Water in Arizona
Government Scouts: Moonlight
A Crow Scout

A Mountain Lion Hunting
Coyotes
Hostiles Watching the Column
Satisfying the Demands of Justice: The Head
Sketch-Book Notes [5 heads]
The Punchers
Riding Herd in the Rain
Mexican Vaqueros Breaking a "Bronc"
A "Sun Fisher"
A Running Bucker
Riding the Range: Winter
Snow Indian, or the Northwest Type
Nez Perce—Indian
A Cheyenne Warrior
A Greaser
A Captain of Infantry in Field Rig
A "Wind Jammer"
Cavalry Column Out of Forage
Half-Breed Horse Thieves of the Northwest
A Misdeal
Over the Foot-Hills
Taking the Robe
Cowboy Leading Calf
Cow Pony Pathos
The Cavalry Cook with Water
A Modern Cavalry Camp
Fox Terriers Fighting a Badger
High Finance at the Cross-Roads
Sketch-Book Notes [4 Indian heads]
The Indian Soldier
The Squaw Pony

U. S. Dragoon, '47
A Scout, 1868
U. S. Cavalry Officer on Campaign
A Reservation Indian
Solitude
The Twilight of the Indian
——, De Luxe Edition. Limited to 250 numbered copies bound in full leather, with inserted publication notice signed by Remington and the publisher; plain gilt-lettered imprint on cover and publisher's initials on back; gilt top, printed on heavy plate paper; boxed; and accompanied by an artist's proof print signed by Remington.

Remington's Frontier Sketches, Introduction by George S. Rowe. The Werner Company, Chicago, 1898. ¶ Black lettering and brown pictorial on cream-colored heavy boards. Oblong 4to. 9½″ x 12½″. Not paginated. Tissues between plates. ¶ Contains 15 Remington plates previously published in "Personal Recollections of General Nelson A. Miles."

Bunch of Buckskins, A. R. H. Russell, N. Y., 1901. ¶ Eight lithograph plates 15″ x 20″ in full color from pastel drawings. Introductory note by Owen Wister, portfolio, original paper label. ¶ Contains: A Cheyenne Buck; A Sioux Chief; A Breed; Old Ramon; A Cavalry Officer; An Army Packer; An Arizona Cowboy; A Trapper.

Western Types. Charles Scribner's Sons, N. Y., 1902. ¶ Set of four f-c. Remington prints, 12″ x 16″: The

Cowboy; The Scout; The Half Breed; The Cossack Post (Cavalryman).

Done in the Open, with introduction by Owen Wister, and verses by Owen Wister and others. R. H. Russell, N. Y., 1902. ¶ Plain lettering and full figure of soldier in color on cream-colored boards; buckram back-strip. First Edition bears R. H. Russell imprint on cover and with caption for the picture "Caught in the Circle" printed in blue and red. Folio, 11½″ x 16½″. Not paginated. ¶ First appearance of Remington pictures noted below:

Cover (soldier with full equipment) f-c
(Small drawing of horse, men and cabins); (Adobe dwelling)
Front., If Skulls Could Speak
Title page (soldier with full equipment)
(Head of an Indian)
(Head of French Canadian)
Introduction tail-piece (soldier lying prone writing)
Mixed Up
The Last Token, d-p
(Head of a soldier)
Artful Dodgers
(Head of Indian in fur cap)
The Red Man's Food
(Head of cowboy)
The Cow Puncher
The Tortoise and the Hare, d-p.
(Horse with saddle)
The Parley
(Head of Indian)
The Pinto
The Quest
Latest News, d-p.
(Head of man)
The Advance
The Last Shot, d-p.
(Head of frontiersman)
A Christmas Carol
(Head of frontiersman)

The Round-Up
(Head of Mexican)
His Own Mount
Oo-yah!, d-p.
(A donkey)
Facts or Fiction
Big Medicine
News From the Front
Mexican Monte, d-p.
Live and Let Die!
(Caught in the Circle, d-p. f-c., from *Collier's*)
(Caribou)
The Long and Short of It
A Little Summer Sault;
(Head of Indian)
No Understand
A Sure Sign, d-p.
Gentlemen in Khaki
(Mule with pack)
Sheep Ranching
(A pueblo house)
The Cayuse
The Smugglers, d-p.
(A whiskered gent)
Ready? Go!
At Last, d-p.
(Head of Indian)
On Okanogan's Banks
The Call to Death
(Head of Indian)
Their Fate
("5,000 Reward, Dead or Alive!" d-p., from *Collier's*)
"Forward, March!"
(Head of frontiersman)
Buenos Noces
(Head of Mexican)
The Rooky
Heroes, d-p.
Tail-piece (Magpie)

——, De Luxe Edition. R. H. Russell, N. Y., 1902. Limited to 250 copies in full leather with inserted publication notice slip signed by Remington and publisher.

——, Variant editions for the same

year of 1902 include Russell imprint but with the changed cover having closed type in the title; also without the Russell imprint on cover; also a P. F. Collier and Son edition.

Remington Portfolio of Drawings. P. F. Collier & Son, 1904. ¶ Decorated boards, tied. ¶ Contains 3 f-c prints 5″ x 7½″ with letter-press advertising set of 12.

Six Remington Prints in Color, P. F. Collier & Son, N. Y., 1904-1908. ¶ Large folio, gray boards, cloth back, paper label. ¶ Contains the following f-c. Remington prints, 11″ x 17″: Gathering of the Trappers; Argument with the Town Marshal; The Bell Mare; The Emigrants; Pony Tracks in the Buffalo Trail; The Buffalo Runners.

Frederic Remington 4 Pictures. P. F. Collier & Son, N. Y., 1906-1907. ¶ Large folio. ¶ Contains the following f-c Remington prints, 14″ x 19¾″: Radisson and Groseilliers; The Howl of the Weather; Downing the Nigh Leader; The Parley. (Also four prints by C. D. Gibson)

Remington's Four Best Paintings. P. F. Collier & Son, N. Y., 1908. ¶ Large envelope, paper label. ¶ Contains following Remington f-c prints, 11″ x 15″ matted 15″ x 20″: Evening on a Canadian Lake; Caught in the Circle; Coming to the Call; His First Lesson.

Remington Portfolio: Eight New Remington Prints. P. F. Collier & Son, N. Y., 1908-1909. ¶ Red boards, cloth back. ¶ Contains following f-c. prints: The Warrior's Last Ride; On the Southern Plains in 1860; The Snow Trail; Indians Simulating Buffalo; With the Eye of the Wind; The Sentinel; The Dead Men; The Pool in the Desert.

Books, Etc. Illustrated or Containing Pictures by Frederic Remington

American Art by American Artists. P. F. Collier & Son, N. Y., 1914. ¶ Oblong folio, 12½″ x 16⅝″; paper label on dark-blue cloth. ¶ Contains 8 f-p. f-c. plates and 4 f-p., black-and-white plates by Remington from *Collier's.*

American Art Galleries. *Works of*

Frederic Remington (Catalog). Sold at Auction, Jan. 13, 1893. ¶ Slate lettering and sketch on white paper wrapper; not paginated. 5½″ x 7″. ¶ 5 Remington sketches:
Cover (Indian head); Title page (Cowboy on bucking bronco); (Indian on horse, rear view);

(Indian on horse, front view); Tail-piece (Prussian officer).
Baylor, Frances C. *Juan and Juanita.* Houghton, Mifflin & Co., Boston, 1888. ¶ Gilt lettering and brown pictorial on green cloth. 8vo. 6¾″ x 8⁹⁄₁₆″. ¶ 2 Remington illus. from *St. Nicholas.* ¶ Scarce.

Becholdt, Frederick R. *Tales of the Old Timers.* The Century Co., N. Y. 1924. ¶ Cloth; 12mo. ¶ Cover design and front. by Remington.

Bigelow, Poultney. *The Borderland of Czar and Kaiser.* Harper & Brothers, N. Y., copyright 1894, published 1895. ¶ Gilt lettering and gilt-colored design on black, and black design on gilt-colored cloth. 12mo. 5″ x 7½″. ¶ 69 Remington illus. from *H. M.*

Bigelow, Poultney. *White Man's Africa.* Harper & Brothers, N. Y., 1898. ¶ Gilt lettering and colored pictorial on gray cloth. 8vo. 5¾″ x 8½″. ¶ 3 Remington illus. from *H. M.*

Boniface, Lieut. Jno. J. *The Cavalry Horse and His Pack.* Hudson-Kimberly Pub. Co., Kansas City, 1903. Gilt lettering and black head of horse design on dark-tan cloth. 8vo. 5½″ x 7¾″. ¶ Front. by Remington.

Book of Bravery. Charles Scribner's Sons, N. Y. 1919. ¶ Cloth, 8vo. ¶ 1 Remington illus.

Brady, Cyrus Townsend. *Indian Fights and Fighters.* Doubleday, Page & Co., N. Y., 1904. ¶ 12mo. ¶ 1 Remington illus.

Briggs, Harold. *Frontiers of the Northwest.* D. Appleton-Century Co., N. Y., 1940. ¶ 8vo. brown cloth. ¶ 1 Remington illus.

Brooks, Elfridge S. *The Century Book for Young Americans.* The Century Co., N. Y., 1893. ¶ Pictorial cloth; 4to. 7½″ x 9¾″. ¶ 2 Remington illus.

Brown, Henry Collins. *In the Golden Nineties.* (Valentine's Manual No. 12), Valentine's Manual, Inc. Hastings-on-Hudson, 1928. ¶ Gilt lettering on dark-blue cloth. 12mo. 5½″ x 8¼″. ¶ 1 Remington illus. from *H. W.*

Calkins, Frank W. *Tales of the West.* Donohue, Henneberry & Co., Chicago, 1893. ¶ Pictorial dark-brown cloth. 8vo. Several, separately paginated parts. Comes in variant bindings, arrangement of stories and sizes 5½″ x 7⅞″ to 6″ x 9″; with no priority established. ¶ 2 Remington illus. from *Youth's Companion.*

Carter, Lieut. Col. W. H. *From Yorktown to Santiago.* The Lord Baltimore Press, Baltimore, 1900. ¶ Pictorial, light-yellow cloth; gilt top. 8vo. 6¼″ x 9¼″. ¶ 3 Remington illus. and 2 illus. "after Remington by C. H. Ourand."

Carter, Gen. W. H. *Old Army Sketches.* The Lord Baltimore Press, Baltimore, 1906. ¶ Gold lettering on dark-blue cloth; gilt top. 8 vo. 5½″ x 8″. ¶ 1 Remington illus. and 3 illus. "after Remington by C. H. Ourand."

Child, Theodore. *Spanish-American Republics.* Harper & Brothers, N. Y., 1891. ¶ Pictorial and gilt on blue-green cloth. 4to. 7¾″ x 11″. ¶ 3 Remington illus.

Cody, Buffalo Bill (William F.). *Story of the Wild West.* Historical Pub. Co., Phila., 1888. ¶ Pictorial brown cloth. Also comes in gaudy pictorial on pea-green cloth. Thick 12mo. 6½″ x 9″. ¶ 2 Remington illus.

Connor, Ralph. *The Patrol of the Sun Dance.* Hodder & Stoughton, London, 1914. ¶ 8vo. ¶ The American edition contains no Remington illus.

Creelman, James. *On The Great Highway.* Lothrop Pub. Co., Boston, October 9, 1901. ¶ Gilt lettering and design on red cloth. 12mo. 5½″ x 7¾″. ¶ 1 Remington illus.:

The Charge at El Caney, f-p. 198.

Custer, Elizabeth B. *Following the Guidon.* Harper & Brothers, N. Y., 1890. ¶ Gilt lettering and flags on green cloth. 12mo. 5″ x 7½″. ¶ 2 Remington illus.

Custer, Elizabeth B. *Tenting on the Plains.* Charles L. Webster & Co., N. Y., 1887. ¶ Variable bindings. Gilt lettering and flags on green cloth. 8vo. 6″ x 9¼″. ¶ 11 Remington illus.:

"Stand There, Cowards, Will You . . .?" f-p. 295; Conestoga Wagon, or Prairie-Schooner, f-p. 351; The Officer's Dress . . ., f-p. 375; A Suspended Equestrienne, f-p. 387; Whipping Horses to Keep Them from Freezing, f-p. 497; "Well, You Are a Warm-blooded Cuss," f-p. 523; Smoking the Pipe of Peace, f-p. 557; A Buffalo Undecided . . ., f-p. 567; The Addled Letter-Carrier, f-p. 673; Negroes Form Their Own Picket-Line, f-p. 678; An Attack On a Stage-Coach, f-p. 683.

Davis, Richard Harding. *Cuba in War Time.* R. H. Russell, N. Y., 1897. ¶ Black and brown printing on dark-gray boards; deckle edges, gilt top; 12mo. 5¼″ x 7⅝″. Also published in paper wrappers. ¶ First Edition has p. 120 wrongly numbered 119.

¶ 20 f-p. Remington illus. from *New York Journal.*

——. Copyright 1898. ¶ With back-pocket (10″ x 28½″) war map of Cuba, Porto Rico and Philippines, with cut-out flags of U. S., Spain and Cuba for following progress of the war.

Davis, Richard Harding. *Notes of a War Correspondent.* Charles Scribner's Sons, N. Y., 1910. ¶ Gilt lettering on maroon cloth. 12mo. 1 Remington illus.

Davis, Richard Harding. *Ranson's Folly.* Charles Scribner's Sons, N. Y., July 1902. ¶ Gilt lettering and colored picture on light-wine cloth; gilt top; 12mo. 5¼″ x 7⅞″. ¶ First issue with folio number on p. 345. ¶ 3 Remington illus. from *Collier's.*

Davis, Richard Harding. *The West from a Car Window.* Harper & Brothers, N. Y., 1892. ¶ Silver lettering on blue cloth. 12mo. 5¼″ x 7½″. ¶ 20 Remington illus. from *H. W.*

Davis, Richard Harding. *A Year from a Reporter's Note Book.* Harper & Brothers, N. Y., copyright 1897, pub. 1898. ¶ Red lettering on gray paper boards; 12mo. 5¼″ x 7½″. ¶ 4 Remington illus. from *H. W.*

Decker, Karl. *The Story of Evangelina Cisneros.* Continental Pub. Co., N. Y., copyright 1897, pub. 1898. ¶ Gilt and black lettering on green cloth; gilt top; (also issued in large paper uncut 12mo.) 12mo. 5″ x 7⅝″. ¶ 4 Remington illus. from *New York Journal.*

Dodge, Theodore Ayrault. *Riders of Many Lands.* Harper & Brothers, N. Y., copyright 1893, pub. 1894. ¶ Gilt lettering and silver spur design on light-brown cloth; gilt top; 8vo. 6¼″ x 9¼″. ¶ 17 Remington illus. from *H. M.*

——. English Edition. Harper & Brothers, London, 1894.

Downey, Fairfax. *Indian Fighting Army.* Charles Scribner's Sons, N. Y., 1941. ¶ Gilt lettering on blue cloth. 8vo. ¶ First Edition has "A" on copyright page. ¶ Contains 39 Remington illus.

Eggleston, Edward. *The Household History of the United States.* D. Appleton & Co., N. Y., copyright 1888, pub. 1889. ¶ Gilt lettering and pictorial design on slate cloth; 8vo. 6½″ x 8¾″. 3 Remington illus.:

Indian Kindling Fire, p. 75; Pack-Horses, p. 95; Battle of Washita, p. 363.

Ellis, Edward S. *True Stories of the American Indians*. W. E. Scull, n.p., 1905. ¶ Red, blue and gilt lettering and colored picture on blue cloth, 8vo. 7¼″ x 9¾″. ¶ 2 Remington illus.

Emerson, Edwin Jr. *A History of the Nineteenth Century*. P. F. Collier & Son, N. Y., copyright 1900, pub. 1901. 3 vols. ¶ Gilt lettering on dark-red cloth; 12mo. 5⅞″ x 8″. ¶ 1 Remington illus. in f-c. from *Scribner's*.

Field, Eugene. *Field Flowers*. Pub. by Mrs. Eugene Field & Monument Committee, 1896. ¶ Green lettering and green-and-wine design on white buckram; 8vo. 8″ x 10¾″. ¶ Prospectus for book laid in. Not paginated. ¶ 2 Remington illus.

French, L. A. *The Desertion of Sergeant Cobb*. Knickerbocker Press, N. Y., n.d. ¶ Boards, vellum back. 4to. Contains front. by Remington, date 1901.

Fry, James B. *Army Sacrifices*. D. Van Nostrand, N. Y., 1887. ¶ Gilt lettering on slate-blue cloth. Title on cover "Indian Fights, 1887"; 12mo. 4¾″ x 6¾″. ¶ Scarce. ¶ 3 Remington illus.:
The Island of Death, p. 17; He Curses the Apache, p. 162; A Daring Plunge, p. 181.

Garland, Hamlin. *The Book of the American Indian*. Harper & Brothers, N. Y., 1923. ¶ Black lettering and appliqued brown print of Indian head, on brown paper boards; gilt lettering on black cloth backstrip; 4to. 9⅛″ x 12½″. Box: brown lettering and Indian head on cream colored paper label. Dust wrapper: Black letter and f-c. Indian on horse (from *A Bunch of Buckskins*) on brown paper. ¶ Contains 37 Remington illus. including 4 f-c. plates from *A Bunch of Buckskins*.

Godfrey, Edward S. *Gen. George A. Custer and the Battle of Little Big Horn*. The Century Co., 1908. ¶ 38-page pamphlet, paper wrappers. ¶ 5 Remington illus.

Gould, A. C., ed. *Sport; or Shooting or Fishing*. Bradlee, Whidden Pub. Co., Boston, 1889. ¶ Cloth-bound portfolio. Plates 12″ x 18″. ¶ 2 f-c. plates by Remington:
Antelope Hunting; Goose Shooting

Griffin, Solomon Buckley. *Mexico of Today*. Harper & Brothers, N. Y., 1886. ¶ Silver lettering and silver-and-brown design on light-brown cloth; 12mo. 5¼″ x 7⅝″. ¶ First book containing Remington illus. ¶ 2 Remington illus. (unsigned):
Mexican Custom-House Guard, p. 11; Mexican Soldier on Guard, p. 101

Gunnison, Almon. *Wayside and Fireside Rambles*. Universalist Publishing House, Boston, copyright 1893, pub. 1894. ¶ Gilt lettering on blue cloth; 12mo. 5¼″ x 7⅝″. ¶ 7 Remington illus.:
(Orator John), p. 11; (Professor and Student), p. 86; (Cleaning House), p. 123; (With the rank of Captain), p. 186; (Parson and small boy), p. 206; (Stocking at the Chimney), p. 222; (Last night in the old house), p. 232

Harper's Encyclopaedia of United States History. (Based on plan by Benson John Lossing), Harper & Brothers, N. Y., 1905. 10 vols. ¶ 8vo.

Harper's Pictorial History of the War in the Philippines. Marion Wilcox, ed. Harper & Brothers, N. Y., 1900. ¶ Gilt lettering on gray-green cloth and black leather; folio 12″ x 16¼″. ¶ 1 Remington illus.:
General Lawton, f-p. f-c. 325

Harper's Pictorial History of the War with Spain. With an introduction by Maj. Gen. Nelson A. Miles; Harper & Brothers, N. Y., 1899. 32 parts—black lettering and pictorial on brown-paper wrappers; small folio 12″ x 17″. ¶ 21 illus. and 2 articles by Remington, from *H. M.* First Edition also issued bound in pictorial cloth.

Harte, Bret. *The Luck of the Roaring Camp and Other Tales*. Vol. I, *The Writings of Bret Harte*. Houghton, Mifflin & Co., Boston, 1896. ¶ Gilt lettering and design on slate-green cloth; gilt top; 12mo. 5½″ x 8¼″. ¶ 1 Remington illus.:
"He Rastled With My Finger," f-p. 6

Harte, Bret. *Maruja and Other Tales*. Vol. V, *The Writings of Bret Harte*, Houghton, Mifflin & Co., Boston, 1896. ¶ Gilt lettering and design on slate-green cloth; gilt top; 12mo. 5½″ x 8¼″. ¶ 1 Remington illus.:
Don Jose Sepulvida and Bucking Bob, front.

Harte, Bret. *Poems and Two Men of Sandy Bar*. Vol. XII, *The Writings of Bret Harte*, Houghton, Mifflin & Co., Boston, 1896. ¶ Gilt lettering and design on slate-green cloth; gilt top; 12mo. 5½″ x 8¼″. ¶ 1 Remington illus.:
"An Animal That was Extremely Rare," f-p. 132

Harte, Bret. *Tales of the Argonauts*. Vol. II, *The Writings of Bret Harte*, Houghton, Mifflin & Co., Boston, 1896. Gilt lettering and design on slate-green cloth; gilt top; 12mo. 5½″ x 8¼″. ¶ 1 Remington illus.:
The Two Opponents Came Nearer, p. 4

Hawthorne, Julian. *History of the United States*. P. F. Collier & Son, N. Y., 1910. 3 vols. ¶ Gilt lettering on blue cloth; 12mo. 5⅝″ x 8″. ¶ 2 Remington f-c. f-p. plates from *Collier's*.

Hill, Dean. *Football Thru the Years*. Gridiron Publishing Co., N. Y., 1940. ¶ Green cloth; 4to. 9⅛″ x 12¼″. ¶ 17 Remington illus.

Hough, Emerson. *The Way to the West*. The Bobbs-Merrill Co., Indianapolis, 1903. ¶ Gilt lettering and blue-and-white design on gray cloth; 12mo. 5¼″ x 7⅝″. ¶ 5 Remington illus.

Howard, Maj. Gen. O. O. *Famous Indian Chiefs I Have Known*. Century Co., N. Y., 1908. ¶ Black lettering and pictorial with blue decoration, red-brown cloth; 12mo. 5⅜″ x 7¾″. ¶ 2 Remington illus.

Howard, Maj. Gen. O. O. *My Experiences Among Our Hostile Indians*. A. D. Worthington & Co., Hartford, 1907. ¶ Gilt lettering on embossed blue cloth; 8vo. 6″ x 9″. ¶ 12 Remington illus.

Humfreville, J. Lee. *Twenty Years Among Our Savage Indians*. The Hartford Pub. Co., Hartford, 1897. Sold only to subscribers. ¶ Pictorial cloth. 8vo. 6″ x 8½″. ¶ 46 Remington illus. including 2 originals:
Going to the Sun Dance, p. 412; Indians Returning to Their Camp from a Fall Buffalo Hunt, f-p. 625

Illustrators, Annual of the Society of, Introduction by Royal Cortissoz. Charles Scribner's Sons, N. Y., 1911. ¶ Gilt lettering on brown paper covered boards; 4to. 9¼″ x 11¼″. ¶ 1

Remington illus.:
(Sketch of man on horse)

Inman, Col. Henry. *The Old Santa Fe Trail*. The Macmillan Co., N. Y., 1897. ¶ Gilt lettering and colored pictorial on green buckram; 8vo. 6″ x 9″. ¶ 9 Remington illus., incl. 5 not previously pub.:

Title page (Buffalo); A Pack Train to Santa Fe, 1820, f-p. 57; Troops Going to Mexico, 1847, f-p. 109; A Buffalo with the Pack, f-p. 209; A Trapper and His Pony, f-p. 485

Issacson, Robert. *Frederic Remington— A Painter of American* Life. Privately printed, N. Y., 1943. ¶ 4to. in slip case. Limited to 500 copies.

Janvier, Thomas A. (and others). *The Armies of Today*. Harper & Brothers, N. Y., 1892. ¶ Gilt lettering and design on green cloth; gilt top; 8vo. 6¼″ x 9 5/16″. ¶ 14 Remington illus. from *H. M.*

Janvier, Thomas A. *The Aztec Treasure House*. Harper & Brothers, N. Y., 1890. ¶ Gilt lettering and design on slate-green cloth; 12mo. 5¼″ x 7⅛″. ¶ 19 Remington illus. from *H. W.*

King, Gen. Charles. *An Apache Princess*. The Hobart Co., N. Y., Sept. 1903. ¶ White-and-red lettering, and black-and-red design on red cloth; 12mo. 5⅛″ x 7½″. Also comes with gilt lettering, and photo of Indian girl in f-c. on paper label on red cloth; gilt top; same size. No priority established. ¶ 1 Remington illus.:

The Fight in the Cañon, front. (also on p. 220)

King, Gen. Charles. *A Daughter of the Sioux*. The Hobart Co., N. Y., March 15, 1903. Same variant bindings as for *An Apache Princess*; 12mo. 5⅛″ x 7½″. ¶ 3 Remington illus.:

Ray's Troops, front. (also p. 72); The Major Sought to Block that Morning's Ride in Vain, p. 21; "The Soldier Leaped from His Saddle," p. 94

King, Gen. Charles. *To the Front*. Harper & Brothers, N. Y., 1908. ¶ White lettering and two-tone blue pictorial design on light-brown cloth; 12mo. 5⅛″ x 7⅝″. ¶ 4 Remington illus. from *H. M.*

Lamb's (Club) Star Gambol (program). May 1898. ¶ Printed paper wrappers. 4to. ¶ 1 original Remington illus.:
"Elevating the Stage Coach"

Lamb's (Club) Star Gambol (program). 1916. ¶ Colored pictorial paper wrappers; 4to. 1 original Remington illus.:
"I Drink with My Left Hand— Pard—Savy"

Laut, A. C. *Pathfinders of the West*. The Macmillan Co., N. Y., Nov. 1904. ¶ White lettering and white-and-gilt design on dark-green cloth; gilt top; 12mo. 5¾″ x 8⅛″. ¶ 4 Remington illus. from *Century*.

Lewis, Alfred Henry. *The Black Lion Inn*. R. H. Russell, N. Y., May, 1903. ¶ Black-and-red lettering and design on light-yellow cloth; 12mo. 5⅛″ x 7⅝″. ¶ 15 Remington illus. from *Drawings* and *Done in the Open*.

Lewis, Alfred Henry. *Wolfville*. Frederick A. Stokes Co., N. Y., 1897. ¶ Gilt-and-black lettering and white-and-brown pictorial on orange-yellow cloth; 12mo. 5¼″ x 7⅝″. Also comes in red cloth. ¶ 21 Remington illus.:

Cover illustration (Westerner firing two six-shooters); front., "An' They Leaves Him Thar on the Trail"; Title page illustration (Texas Thompson); The Old Cattleman, f-p. 1; Wolfville, f-p. 3; Doc Peters, f-p. 7; Cherokee Hall, f-p. 9; Old Man Enright, f-p. 31; "This Yere's Thoughtful of Jack," f-p. 56; "He's Shore a Fash'nable Lookin' Injun," f-p. 87; "An' They Leaves Him Thar on the Trail," f-p. 115; Texas Thompson, p. 120 (same as title page); Old Monte, f-p. 135; "He Lays Thar Rollin' His Eyes," f-p. 146; "That He'pless Shorthorn Stops Both Heels," p. 172; "It's on the Spring Round-up," f-p. 203; "Natcherally I Stops an' Surveys Him Careful," p. 227; "Them Three Mexicans is Eliminated," f-p. 268; "The Red Dog Chief," p. 278; Crawfish Jim, p. 328; Tail-piece (wooden grave marker), p. 237.

Lewis, Alfred Henry. *Wolfville Days*. Frederick A. Stokes Co., N. Y., 1902. ¶ Gilt lettering and colored pictorial on red cloth; 12 mo. 5⅛″ x 7½″. ¶ 1 Remington illus.:
Front., "Hands Up"

Longfellow, Henry Wadsworth. *The Song of Hiawatha*. Houghton, Mifflin & Co., Boston, copyright 1890, pub. 1891. ¶ Three issues of First Edition: full vellum with gilt stamped lettering and design, gilt top, limited to 250

copies—full suede with gilt stamped and top—and cloth; 8vo. ¶ 22 f-p. photogravures and 379 text illus. by Remington.

Photogravures:

All the Tribes Beheld the Signal, p. 8; Like a Ghost That Goes at Sunrise, p. 18; Then Upon One Knee Uprising, p. 32; Glared Like Ishkoodch, the Comet, p. 38; And He Saw a Youth Approaching, p. 50; Pitched It Sheer Into the River, p. 64; Thus the Birch Canoe Was Builded, p. 70; Long Sat Waiting for an Answer, p. 76; Then Began the Greatest Battle, p. 90; "I Will Follow You, My Husband!", p. 102; Through the Shadows and the Sunshine, p. 112; "And her lovers, the rejected . . .," p. 120; " 'Twas the Women Who in Autumn," p. 134; Such as These the Shapes They Painted, p. 146; "I Can Blow You Strong, My Brother," p. 156; All the Old Men and the Young Men . . ., p. 164; Through Bush, and Brake, and Forest, p. 172; Sideways Fell Into the River, p. 188; Sat Down in the Farthest Corner, p. 194; Then He Sat Down, Still and Speechless, p. 204; "Sit Here by the Dying Embers," p. 210; Came the Black-Robe Chief . . . the Pale-Face, p. 220

Text Illustrations:

Deer, p. iii; Chippewa baby basket, p. xii; Indian dog, p. xiii; Cheyenne Indian flute, p. xviii; Blue heron, p. 1; Fox, p. 2; Grouse, p. 2; Warrior, p. 3; Pawnie headdress, p. 3; Deer, p. 4; Baby basket, p. 4; War club, p. 5; Blackfoot moccasin, p. 5; Rocky Mountains, p. 6; Calumet and fire-bag, p. 7; Fire stick, p. 7; Warrior, p. 8; Sioux hatchet and fire-bag, p. 9; Hand, p. 9; Shell hatchet, p. 10; Fire-bag, p. 10; Headdress, p. 11; Blackfoot war shirt, p. 11; Squaw, p. 12; Calumet, p. 12; River bank, p. 13; Decorated buffalo skin, p. 14; Bear, p. 14; Bear, p. 15; Tomahawk, p. 16; Legging and moccasin, p. 17; Warrior, p. 17; Snow-shoe, p. 18; Blackfoot legging, p. 19; Bow and arrows, p. 20; Shield and lance, p. 21; Pipe, p. 22; Woman's belt, p. 23; War shirt, p. 23; Squaw, p. 24; Indian camp, p. 25; Coup-stick, p. 25; Boy, p. 26; Snake Indian papoose

Comanche moccasin, p. 206; Indian chair, p. 206; Old wooden dish, p. 207; Pipe head, p. 208; Paddle, p. 208; Omaha calumet, p. 209; Image, p. 210; Headdress, horse-hair, p. 210; Sword and club, p. 211; Shield, p. 211; Bow case and quiver, p. 212; Cheyenne moccasin, p. 213; Papago olla, p. 213; Helmeted soldier, p. 214; Blunderbuss, bow and arrow, p. 214; Blackfoot gun case, p. 215; Colonial head, p. 216; Trader's head, p. 216; River view, p. 217; Pipe, arrow and lance, p. 218; Pottery, p. 219; Shield, p. 219; Headdress, p. 220; Willow basket, p. 220; Priest's head, p. 221; Shirt, p. 221; Priest, p. 222; Birch-bark vessel, p. 223; Pottery, p. 223; Medicine spear, p. 224; Pottery, p. 224; Ideal head, p. 225; Medicine wand, p. 226; Wild ducks, p. 226; War club, p. 227; Antique ornament, p. 227; Papago carrying basket, p. 228; Hunter's cabin, p. 229; Papago mask, p. 230; Quirt, p. 231; Blackfoot packing bag, p. 231; Whip, p. 232; Pack, p. 232; Baby basket, p. 233; Blackfoot squaw saddle, p. 233; Pottery, p. 233; Apache fiddle, p. 234; Pottery, p. 235; Trader's hatchet, p. 236; Elk-horn riding whip, p. 237; Tom-tom, p. 237; Buffalo skull, p. 238; Pottery, p. 238; Stone axe, p. 239; Cheyenne elk-horn saddle, p. 239; Gourd cup, p. 240; Zuni jug, p. 240; Cheyenne baby basket, p. 241; Ideal head, p. 242; Peace-pipe, p. 242.

——, Remington-Parrish-Wyeth English Edition. George G. Harrap & Co., Ltd., London, 1911. ¶ Full leather, embossed cover design by Maxfield Parrish; gilt top; uncut; 8vo. 7⅜″ x 9⅝″. ¶ Frontispiece by N. C. Wyeth; the balance of illustration by Frederic Remington as in the original edition.

McCracken, Harold. *Pershing—The Story of a Great Soldier*. Brewer & Warren, N. Y., 1931. ¶ Red lettering on blue field, on red cloth; 12mo. 5⅝″ x 8⅛″. ¶ 4 Remington illus. from *H. M.*

Mabie, Hamilton W. *The Story of America*. John C. Winston & Co., Phila., 1892. ¶ Gilt lettering on wine-colored cloth and brown ¾ leather; 4to. 7¾″ x 10⅜″. ¶ 5 Remington illus. Later editions have variant titles.

Miles, Gen. Nelson A. *Personal Recollections of . . .* The Werner Company, Chicago, 1896. ¶ Gilt lettering and gilt-and-silver pictorial design on brown cloth; 4to. 7⅝″ x 10″. ¶ 15 Remington illus.:
　Sioux Warriors, f-p. 79; Soldiers Opening Their Veins for Want of Water, f-p. 111; Indian Village Routed, f-p. 161; Twenty-five to One, f-p. 177; General Miles' Envoy to the Hostiles on the Staked Plains, f-p. 189; Meeting Between the Lines, f-p. 223; Captain Baldwin Hunting the Hostile Camp, f-p. 233; Indians Firing the Prairie, f-p. 245; The Crazy Horse Fight, f-p. 257; Pursuing the Indians, f-p. 269; The Lame Deer Fight, f-p. 281; Mounting the Infantry on Captured Ponies, f-p. 291; Fighting Over the Captured Herd, f-p. 307; Surrender of Chief Joseph, f-p. 331; Lawton's Pursuit of Geronimo, f-p. 515

——. Full leather. ¶ Later issues of this book carry front. wording "Major General Miles."

Mahan, Capt. A. T. *The War in South Africa*. Peter Fenelon Collier & Son, N. Y., 1900. ¶ Gilt letter on dark-blue cloth; oblong folio 11½″ x 17¼″. ¶ 1 Remington f-p. f-c. plate: General French's Irregulars Harassing the Boers After the Relief of Kimberly, p. 145

Miller, Joaquin, and others. *Western Frontier Stories*. 1907. ¶ 12mo. (Not examined.)

Millis, Walter. *The Martial Spirit*. Houghton, Mifflin Co., Boston, 1931; Literary Guild, N. Y. ¶ Gilt lettering on wine-colored buckram; 8vo. 6″ x 9″. ¶ 1 Remington illus. from *New York Journal*.

Moore, Charles M. *The Northwest Under Two Flags*. Harper & Brothers, N. Y., 1900. ¶ Dark-brown lettering and black Indian head design on light-brown cloth; 8vo. 5½″ x 8¼″. ¶ 10 Remington illus. from *H. M.*

Morris, Charles. *The Greater Republic*. W. E. Scull, n.p., 1899. ¶ Gilt lettering and design on green cloth; large 8vo. 7½″ x 9¾″. ¶ 2 Remington illus. from *Century*.

Muir, John, ed. *Picturesque California*. J. Dewing Pub. Co., San Francisco, 1888. 10 vols. ¶ Pictorial gray cloth covers. India Proof Edition. Limited and numbered; some plates on satin.

Folio 14½″ x 19⅜″. ¶ 5 Remington illus.:
　Mule Train Crossing the Sierras, f-p., photogravure, 28; Branding Cattle, f-p., photogravure, 184; Miners Prospecting for Gold, f-p., photogravure, 236; Old-Time Types [5 heads], p. 238; A Navajo Sheep-Herder, f p., photogravure, 320

——. Trade Edition. Pictorial blue cloth. Folio 12½″ x 16½″.

——. Two-volume edition, bound in cloth. ¶ No priority established for variant editions.

National Academy of Design. *Illustrated Catalogue*, 74th Annual Exhibition. The Knickerbocker Press, N. Y., April 1899. ¶ 1 Remington illus.: "Missing," No. 306, p. 50

Norris, Frank. *A Deal in Wheat*. Doubleday, Page & Co., N. Y., 1903. ¶ Gilt lettering on red cloth; gilt top; uncut; 12mo. 5½″ x 8¼″. Also without gilt decoration on or top and cut on three sides. ¶ 1 Remington illus. from *Collier's*.

Outing, Short Stories from. Outing Publishing Co., N. Y., 1895. ¶ Contains "Fidele," by Alfred A. Gardner, with 4 Remington illus. from *Outing*.

Pageant of America, The. Ed. by Clark Wissler and others. Yale Univ. Press, New Haven, 1925-1929. 15 vols. ¶ Gilt lettering and design on blue cloth, ¾ levant; 4to. 7⅞″ x 10¼″.
　Vol. I, 8 Remington illus.
　Vol. II, 25 Remington illus. (p. 177, "Pike's Capture" should be titled "The Spanish Escort.")
　Vol. III, 3 Remington illus. (p. 180, "The Stampede" should be titled "Stampeded by Lightning.")
　Vol. IV, 1 Remington illus. (p. 223, "Attack on a Mail Coach" should be titled "Downing the Nigh Leader.")
　Vol. VI, 2 Remington illus.
　Vol. XII, 1 Remington illus.
　Vol. XV, 2 Remington illus.

Parkman, Francis. *The Oregon Trail*. Little, Brown & Co., Boston, 1892. ¶ Gilt lettering and gilt-and-colored design on gold-colored cloth; gilt top; 8vo. 6¼″ x 9″. ¶ 77 Remington illus.:
　Front. (Immigrant train crossing plains); (Frontiersman shooting buffalo), p. 1; Tail-piece (Flint-lock pistol), p. 9; (Frontiersman on horse), p. 11; (Mule hitched to

prairie cart), f-p. 13; (Frontier packer with mules), p. 15; (Indian on horse), p. 22; Tail-piece (Horse with pack saddle), p. 24; Tail-piece (Muzzle-loader gun, powder horn and pouch), p. 28; (Mounted trooper in dress uniform), p. 40; Tail-piece (River and hills), p. 54; (Coyote and human skull), p. 56; (Head of frontier packer), p. 58; (Buffalo and buffalo skull), p. 66; Tail-piece (Flint-lock gun), p. 69; (Head of bearded frontiersman), p. 75; Tail-piece (Horse's head), p. 85; (Indian standing by horse), p. 95; (Head of Indian), p. 103; (Frontiersman and group of half-breeds at Fort Laramie), f-p. 104; (Head of Indian), p. 106; (Crow Indians desecrating the dead), f-p. 108; (Head of Frontiersman), p. 109; (Indian pony and travois), p. 112; (Head of Frontiersman), p. 114; (Muzzle-loader gun and two powder horns), p. 118; (Head of Indian), p. 121; (Saddle), p. 124; (French Canadian in winter clothes), p. 131; (Frontiersman with gun), p. 133; (Head of Indian), p. 136; (Frontiersman with gun), p. 137; (Shoeing a horse), f-p. 140; (Old Indian leading horse with travois), p. 147; (Head of Indian), p. 158; (Mounted Indian with war-bonnet and spear; village), f-p. 160; (Head of half-breed), p. 167; (Old trapper on his horse), p. 170; (Indian racing on horseback), p. 173; (Head of half-breed), p. 175; (Head of frontiersman), p. 176; (Head of Indian), p. 178; (Frontiersman on horse), f-p. 187; (Pinto pony with Indian saddle), p. 204; (Indians firing gun, arrow and beating tom-tom), f-p. 208; (Indian horse with papoose, etc.), p. 217; Mounted Indian at edge of bluff), p. 226; (Wounded buffalo followed by wolves), p. 229; (Mounted Indian on running horse), p. 233; (End of the buffalo hunt), f-p. 236; (Head of Indian woman), p. 243; (Indian medicine man and dog), p. 245; (Head of Indian with feathers in hair), p. 250; (Mounted Indian chief with war axe), p. 255; Tail-piece (Indian drawing of mounted war chief), p. 257; (Indian pipe and bag), p. 259; (Head of frontiersman), p. 262; (Indian pack train

coming through mountains), f-p. 268; (Head of frontiersman), p. 271; (Head of Indian), f-p. 281; (Indian with pipe, in hills), p. 286; (Two horsemen beside creek in hills), f-p. 292; (Three horses grazing), p. 306; (Head of frontiersman), p. 312; (Head of trader), p. 315; (Head of Indian), p. 327; (Head of French Canadian), p. 328; (Head of frontiersman), p. 330; Tail-piece (Spurs), p. 336; (Head of emigrant), p. 337; (Mexican and horse), p. 340; (Driving horses), p. 343; (Emigrant on mule), p. 345; Tail-piece (Quirt), p. 355; (Mounted frontiersman loading muzzle-loader at gallop), p. 358; (Buffalo hunter riding down steep bank), f-p. 365; (Head of frontiersman), p. 387

——. Full leather, decorated.

——. Wyeth-Remington Edition, 1925. ¶ Edition limited to 975 numbered copies. ¶ Gilt lettering on ¾ red cloth, and brown picture on pale-brown paper boards; gilt top; 8vo. 6⅜″ x 9⅜″. ¶ 5 Remington illus. from original edition. No Remingtons in the trade edition of this issue.

Pennell, Joseph. *Modern Illustration.* Chiswick Press, London, 1895. ¶ Printed wrappers, 8vo. ¶ Limited to 125 copies on Japanese vellum. ¶ 1 Remington illus.

Pennell, Joseph. *Pen Drawing and Pen Draughtsmen.* Macmillan & Co., N. Y., 1894. ¶ Gilt lettering on slate-green cloth; 4to. 9½″ x 11¾″. ¶ 1 Remington illus. from *Century.*

Powell, E. Alexander. *Gentlemen Rovers.* Charles Scribner's Sons, N. Y., Sept. 1913. ¶ Gilt lettering on red cloth; 12mo. 5¾″ x 8¼″. ¶ 1 Remington illus. from *Collier's.*

Ralph, Julian. *Dixie or Southern Scenes and Sketches.* Harper & Brothers, N. Y., copyright 1895, pub. 1896. ¶ Gilt lettering and gilt-and-silver design on green-gray cloth; 8vo. 6⅛″ x 9″. ¶ 10 Remington illus. from *H. M.*

Ralph, Julian. *On Canada's Frontier.* Harper & Brothers, N. Y., 1892. ¶ Gilt lettering and gilt-and-black design on red-brown cloth; 8vo. 6⅛″ x 9″. ¶ 66 Remington illus. from *H. M.*

Ralph, Julian. *Our Great West.* Harper & Brothers, N. Y., 1893. ¶ Gilt lettering and gilt-and-wine decoration

on wine-gray cloth; 8vo. 6⅛″ x 9″. ¶ 4 Remington illus. from *H. M.*

Robertson, Harrison, and others. *Stories of the South.* Charles Scribner's Sons, N. Y., 1893. ¶ Gilt lettering on dark-wine cloth; gilt top; 16mo. 3½″ x 5⅛″. ¶ Contains "How the Derby Was Won" by Harrison Robertson with 6 Remington illus. from *Scribner's.*

Roe, E. P., and others. *Panther Stories.* The Century Co., N. Y., 1904. ¶ Black-green stencil with design and lettering on tan cloth. 12mo. 5¼″ x 7⅝″. ¶ 2 Remington illus. from *St. Nicholas.*

Roosevelt, Theodore. *Big Game Hunting.* G. P. Putnam's Sons, N. Y., copyright 1898, pub. 1899. ¶ Gilt lettering and gilt design on black-leather label on cream-colored buckram; gilt top; 4to. 8½″ x 11½″. ¶ Limited Edition of 1,000 numbered copies. ¶ (Comprises "Hunting Trips of a Ranchman" and "The Wilderness Hunter.") ¶ Signed portrait front. ¶ 1 Remington illus.

Roosevelt, Theodore. *Good Hunting.* Harper & Brothers, N. Y., Feb. 1907. ¶ Red lettering and pictorial paper label on tan cloth; 12mo. 5⅛″ x 8⅝″. ¶ Consists of series of articles which appeared in *Harper's Round Table,* 1896-1897. ¶ Contains 5 f-p. Remington illus.

Roosevelt, Theodore. *Ranch Life and the Hunting Trail.* The Century Co., N. Y., 1888. ¶ Green lettering and gilt design on dark-gray buckram; gilt all around; heavy boards; 4to. 9⅞″ x 12¼″. ¶ 82 Remington illus. from *Century,* plus following originals:

Title page (Cowboy on horse); (Initial sketch of range bull), p. 3; Tail-piece (Bitt), p. 14; (Initial of log ranch building), p. 15; (Initial of mounted cowboy shooting pistol in air), p. 45; (Initial of wolf), p. 73; Tail-piece (Bitt), p. 79; The Peace Sign, p. 101; (Cowboy making pick-up from running horse), p. 111; An Elk, f-p. 130; (Initial of running antelope), p. 131; A Prong-Horn Buck Visits Camp, p. 138; The Buck Overtaken, p. 141; Tail-piece (Bitt), p. 151; Shot!, p. 161; The White Goat at Home, p. 184; End-piece —Adios

——. 1896. ¶ Green lettering and red design on straw-colored cloth; gilt top;

4to. 7¼″ x 10¾″. ¶ 94 Remington illus. All those appearing in 1888 edition plus twelve additional from *Century*.

——. 1899. ¶ Gilt lettering and design on light-green buckram; gilt top; 4to. 7¼″ x 10¾″.

Roosevelt, Theodore. *The Roughriders*. Charles Scribner's Sons, N. Y., 1899. ¶ Gilt lettering and design on slate-brown cloth; gilt top; 8vo. 5¾″ x 8⅝″. ¶ 1 Remington illus. from *Scribner's.*:

"Charge of the Rough Riders at San Juan."

Roosevelt, Theodore. *Stories of the Great West*. The Century Co., N. Y., June 1909. ¶ Black lettering and design on red cloth; 12mo. 5¼″ x 7⅝″. ¶ 14 Remington illus.

Roosevelt, Theodore. *The Wilderness Hunter*. G. P. Putnam's Sons, N. Y., 1893. ¶ Wine lettering and gilt antelope head on gray cloth; 8vo. 6¼″ x 9⅝″. ¶ 1 Remington illus.

Roosevelt, Theodore. *The Winning of the West*. P. F. Collier & Son, N. Y., n.d. Executive Edition. 4 vols. ¶ Gilt lettering on dark-blue cloth; 12mo. 5¾″ x 8″. ¶ 4 Remington illus. (front. of each volume) from *Collier's*. ¶ In the first issue of above Vol. I, last word, p. 160, is "diame," and p. 161 the first word is "ter."

Seely, Howard. *The Jonah of Lucky Valley* and other stories. Harper & Brothers, N. Y., April, 1892. No. 719, "Monthly Series." ¶ Blue lettering on light-blue paper cover; 12mo. 5⅝″ x 8″. Also issued in cloth-covered boards. ¶ 13 Remington illus. from *H. W.*

Sheldon, George William. *Recent Ideals in American Art*. D. Appleton & Co., N. Y. & London, 1888-1889-1890. ¶ Gilt lettering and pictorial on tooled leather-covered boards; gilt all around; small folio 12¾″ x 16⅝″. ¶ 1 Remington illus.:

"Return of a Blackfoot War Party."

——. Issued in parts.

Smith, F. Hopkins. *American Illustrators*. Charles Scribner's Sons, N. Y., 1892. ¶ 5 parts in board covers. Red lettering and brown design on cream paper; folio 13″ x 17″. ¶ Limited Edition of 1,000 numbered sets. ¶ 2 Remington illus.: 1 colored f-p. plate and 1 black-and-white; portrait. ¶ Also a trade edition.

——. *Discussions on American Art and Artists*. Art Students League, N. Y., n.d. ¶ Full cushioned leather; oblong 4to. ¶ Portrait and 2 Remington sketches, pp. 178 and 181.

Spofford, A. R., Ed. *The Library of Historic Characters and Famous Events*. William Finley & Co., Philadelphia, 1896. 10 vols. ¶ ¾ brown morocco; 8vo. ¶ 1 Remington illus.

Squadron "A" Games (program). New York, Feb. 18, 1897. ¶ Pictorial paper wrappers. ¶ 9 Remington illus. from *H. M.*

Stanley, Henry M. *Slavery and the Slave Trade in Africa*. Harper & Brothers, N. Y., 1893. ¶ Black lettering on white cloth; 16mo. 3⅞″ x 5⅜″. ¶ Also comes in blue cloth. ¶ 6 Remington illus. from *H. M.*

St. Nicholas, Indian Stories Retold from. The Century Co., N. Y., 1905. ¶ Green lettering and purple design on straw-colored cloth. 12mo. 5¼″ x 7⅝″. ¶ Front. and 3 other Remington illus. from *St. Nicholas*.

Stevens, Montague. *Meet Mr. Grizzly*. Univ. of New Mexico Press, N. M., 1943. ¶ 8vo. ¶ 1 Remington illus. from *Harper's*. ¶ Page 28, next to last line, should read "July 1895" instead of "August 1894"; and same error on page 280, 4th par., 3rd line.

Sullivan, Mark. *Our Times*: Vol. I, *The Turn of the Century*. Charles Scribner's Sons, N. Y., March 1926. ¶ Gilt lettering and title imprint on blue cloth; 8vo. 6⅜″ x 9¼″. ¶ 1 f-p. Remington (p. 198) from *Collier's* (wrongly credited to *Life*.)

——. *Our Times*: Vol. IV, *The War Begins, 1909-1914*. Charles Scribner's Sons, N. Y., 1932. ¶ Obituary tribute and 1 Remington illus. from *Collier's*.

Summerhayes, Martha. *Vanished Arizona* (2nd Edition). The Salem Press Co., Salem, Mass., 1911. ¶ White lettering and gilt decoration on dark-blue cloth; 12mo. 5⅜″ x 7¾″. ¶ 2 Remington sketches:

(Caricature of Mrs. Summerhayes and John Ermine), p. 290; (Caricature of Remington on horse), p. 293. ¶ Page 291 lists play *John Ermine* as opening at Globe Theatre, Boston, Sept. 1902; should read "1903." ¶ The first Edition of 1908, and the Lakeside Press Edition of 1939 contain no Remington material.

Tappan, Eva March. *Our Country's Story*. Houghton, Mifflin & Co., Boston, 1902. ¶ Black lettering on gray-green cloth; 12mo. 5⅞″ x 7¾″. ¶ 12 Remington illus.

Thomas, Augustus. *Arizona*. C. H. Russell, N. Y., 1899. ¶ Blue cloth; 5¾″ x 8⅜″. ¶ Cover design by Remington (same as on *Drawings*).

Thomas, Augustus. *The Print of My Remembrance*. Charles Scribner's Sons, N. Y., 1922. ¶ Gilt lettering on green cloth; 8vo. 6⅜″ x 9″. ¶ 2 character sketches by Remington from *Saturday Evening Post* and 1 original: Augustus Thomas, p. 376

Thirty Favorite Paintings By Leading American Artists. P. F. Collier & Son, N. Y., 1908. ¶ Red lettering on gilt-edged pale-pink paper label, on red paper covered boards, with blue-black cloth spine; oblong folio 11¼″ x 16½″. ¶ Front. and 1 other f-p. f-c. plate by Remington from *Collier's*.

Vail, R. W. G. "*Frederic Remington*— Chronicler of the Vanished West." N. Y. Public Library, March 1929. ¶ Paper wrapper pamphlet; 7 pages; 8vo. 7″ x 10″. ¶ Reprint from February (1929) *Bulletin* of N. Y. Public Library. ¶ 3 f-p. Remington illus. from *Drawings* and *Collier's*.

Walworth, Jeannette H. *History of New York in Words of One Syllable*. Bedford, Clarke & Co., Chicago, 1888. ¶ Gilt and black lettering and colored design on light-blue cloth; 8vo. 7½″ x 8¾″. ¶ 1 Remington illus. (p. 110) adapted from "Crow Indians Firing Into the Agency," *H. W.*, Nov. 5, 1887.

Warner, Charles Dudley. *Our Italy*. Harper & Brothers, N. Y., 1891. ¶ Gilt lettering and design on blue-gray and slate cloth; gilt top; 8vo. 7″ x 9⅜″. ¶ 2 Remington illus. from *H. M.*

Water Color Society, American, Annual Exhibit (catalog), 1887. ¶ 1 Remington illus.:

"The Flag of Truce in the Indian Wars"

Water Color Society, American, Annual Exhibit (catalog), 1888. ¶ 1 Remington illus. from *H. W.*

Wetmore, Helen Cody. *Last of the Great Scouts*. The Duluth Press Co., 1899. ¶ Gilt lettering on red cloth; 12mo. 5⅞″ x 8 3/16″. ¶ 2 Remington illus., 1 from *Harper's* and 1 original:

153

Under the Lime Light, f-p. 243. ¶ Another issue of same date lacks this picture

Whitney, Caspar. *On Snow-Shoes to the Barren Grounds.* Harper & Brothers, N. Y., 1896. ¶ Gilt lettering and pictorial label on blue cloth; gilt top; 8vo. 6⅜″ x 9¼″. ¶ 17 f-p. Remington illus. from *H. M.*

Whitney, Casper W. *A Sporting Pilgrimage.* Harper & Brothers, N. Y., copyright 1894, pub. 1895. ¶ Gilt lettering and gilt-and-black design on red cloth, 8vo. 6¼″ x 9″. ¶ 6 Remington illus. from *H. W.*

Willets, Gilson. *Workers of the Nation.* P. F. Collier & Son, N. Y., 1903. 2 vols. ¶ 8vo. blue cloth. ¶ 1 f-p. f-c. Remington illus. from *Collier's.*

Wilson, Woodrow. *A History of the American People.* Harper & Brothers, N. Y., 1902. 5 vols. ¶ Gilt lettering on crimson buckram; gilt top; 8vo. 6⅛″ x 8⅞″. ¶ 3 Remington illus. 2 from *Harper's* and 1 original:
Courier DuBois, XVII Century (Vol. II, p. 14.)

——. Special edition limited to 350 signed sets.

Wister, Owen. *Hank's Woman. (The Writings of Owen Wister.)* The Macmillan Company, N. Y., Sept. 1928. ¶ Gilt lettering and design on backstrip and signature "OW" on front cover, on blue cloth; 12mo. 5¼″ x 7 7/16″. ¶ Front. by Remington from *H. M.*

Wister, Owen. *The Jimmyjohn Boss.* Harper & Brothers, N. Y., 1900. ¶ Gilt lettering and pictorial label

on red cloth; 12mo. 5″ x 7½″. ¶ 6 Remington illus. from *H. M.*

Wister, Owen. *A Journey in Search of Christmas.* Harper & Brothers, N. Y., Oct. 1904. ¶ Gilt lettering, black design and colored pictorial on red cloth; gilt top; 8vo. 6″ x 9″. ¶ 3 f-p. illus. by Remington, from *H. W.*

Wister, Owen. *Lin McLean.* Harper & Brothers, N. Y., 1897. ¶ Gilt lettering and design, and black illus. on red cloth; 12mo. 5⅛″ x 7⅝″.
Front. by Remington from *H. M.*

——. *(The Writings of Owen Wister.)* The Macmillan Company, N. Y., Sept. 1928. ¶ Gilt lettering and design on backstrip, and signature "OW" on cover, on blue cloth; 12mo. 5¼″ x 7 7/16″.
Front. by Remington

Wister, Owen. *Members of the Family. (The Writings of Owen Wister.)* The Macmillan Company, N. Y., Sept. 1928. ¶ Gilt lettering and design on backstrip, and signature "OW" on cover, on blue cloth; 12mo. 5¼″ x 7 7/16″.
Front. by Remington

Wister, Owen. *Red Men and White.* Harper & Brothers, N. Y., copyright 1895, pub. 1896. ¶ Gilt lettering and black picture on red cloth; 12mo. 5⅛″ x 7½″. ¶ 17 Remington illus. from *H. M.*

——. *(The Writings of Owen Wister.)* The Macmillan Company, N. Y., Sept. 1928. ¶ Gilt lettering and design on backstrip and signature "OW" on cover, on blue cloth; 12mo. 5¼″ x 7 7/16″.
Front. by Remington

Wister, Owen. *The Virginian. The Macmillan Company,* N. Y., Oct. 1911. ¶ 8vo. boards. ¶ Limited Edition of 100 copies printed on Japan vellum and signed by author. This is first edition of this book to contain Remington illus. ¶ 10 f-p. Remington illus. from *Collier's* and *H. M.*

——. Trade Edition. ¶ Gilt lettering and gilt-framed full-color paper label of book's frontis illus. by Charles M. Russell, on red cloth; gilt top; 12mo. 5⅜″ x 7⅞″. ¶ 10 f-p. Remington illus. from *Collier's* and *H. M.*

——. *(The Writings of Owen Wister.)* The Macmillan Company, N. Y., Sept. 1928. ¶ Gilt lettering and design on backstrip, and signature "OW" on cover, on blue cloth; 12mo. 5¼″ x 7 7/16″.
Front. by Remington

——. Grosset & Dunlap, N. Y., 1928. ¶ Brown lettering and design on light-green paper label on brown cloth; 12mo. 5½″ x 8″. ¶ Front. and 3 f-p. Remington illus. from *Collier's* and *H. M.*

Wister, Owen. *When West Was West.* The Macmillan Company, N. Y., May 1928. ¶ Gilt lettering on blue cloth; 12mo. 5¼″ x 7⅝″.
Front. by Remington

——. *(The Writings of Owen Wister.)* The Macmillan Company, N. Y., Sept. 1928. ¶ Gilt lettering and design on backstrip, and signature "OW" on cover, on blue cloth; 12mo. 5¼″ x 7 7/16″.
Front. by Remington

Books Containing References to Frederic Remington or His Work

Bigelow, Poultney. *Seventy Summers.* Longmans, Green & Co., 1925. 2 vols.

Bishop, Joseph B. *Theodore Roosevelt and His Time.* Charles Scribner's Sons, N. Y., 1920. 2 vols.

Bolton, Theodore. *American Book Illustrators,* Bowker & Co., 1938.

Card, Helen L. *The Collector's Remington* (Books). Privately printed, Woonsocket, R. I., 1946. ¶ Pamphlet; 100 copies.

Card, Helen L. *The Collector's Remington* (Bronzes). Privately printed, Woonsocket. R. I., 1946. ¶ Pamphlet; 100 copies.

Cortissoz, Royal. *American Artists.* Charles Scribner's Sons, N. Y., 1923.

Davis, Charles Belmont. *Adventures and Letters of Richard Harding Davis.* Charles Scribner's Sons, N. Y., 1917.

Downey, Fairfax. *Richard Harding Davis, His Day.* Charles Scribner's Sons, N. Y., 1933.

Harper, J. Henry. *The House of Harper.* Harper & Brothers, N. Y., 1911.

Isham, Samuel. *The History of American Painting.* The Macmillan Co., N. Y., 1905.

Johnson, Robert Underwood. *Remembered Yesterdays.* Little, Brown & Co., Boston, 1923.

Kaufman, Emma and Anne O'Hagan *Cuba at a Glance.* R. H. Russell,

N. Y., 1898. ¶ Contains lengthy letter by Remington.

Marden, Orison Sweet. *Little Visits with Great Americans.* The Success Co., N. Y., 1903.

Metropolitan Museum of Art. *Bulletin.* July 1939. ¶ Biographical sketch, and photo of "The Bronco Buster," pp. 169-70.

N. Y. State Historical Assoc. *Proceedings,* 1929. ¶ Letters to Poultney Bigelow, pp. 45-52.

Rogers, W. A. *A World Worth While.* Harper & Brothers, 1922.

Stokes, Anson P. *Memorials of Eminent Yale Men.* Yale Univ. Press, New Haven, 1914. 2 vols. ¶ Limited edition of 150 copies; also a regular edition.

Sydenham, Lieut. Alvin H. *Frederic Remington.* A Supplement to: "The Daily Journal of Alvin H. Sydenham." N. Y. Public Library, 1940.

¶ Reprint from Aug. 1940 *Bulletin of N. Y. Public Library,* pp. 609-13.

Vincent, George E., ed. *Theodore W. Miller, Rough Rider.* Privately printed, Akron, O., 1899. ¶ Scarce.

Walsh, Richard J. *The Making of Buffalo Bill.* Bobbs-Merrill Co., Indianapolis, 1928.

Wister, Owen. *Members of the Family.* The Macmillan Co., N. Y., 1911. ¶ In the preface Wister pays tribute to Remington.

Remington Bronzes

The titles and quoted descriptions are taken from the sculptor's own application for copyright. Date given is date of copyright.

"The Bronco Buster": "Equestrian statue of cowboy mounted upon and breaking in wild horse standing on hind feet. Cowboy holding onto horse's mane with left hand while right hand is extended upwards." ¶ October 1, 1895.

"The Wounded Bunkie": Two horses in full gallop, side by side. Each horse carries a cavalryman, one of whom has been wounded and is supported in his saddle and kept from falling by arm of the other trooper. ¶ 14 copies. ¶ July 9, 1896.

"The Wicked Pony": Shows a cowboy who has been thrown and is lying flat on the ground, holding onto bronco's ear with left hand. The bronco is lashing out with hind legs. ¶ December 3, 1898.

"The Scalp": Represents a mounted Indian reining up his horse as he triumphantly holds aloft a scalp which he has taken from a defeated enemy. ¶ December 10, 1898.

"The Norther": "Cowboy on horseback in snow storm. Severe wind blowing from rear. Both man and horse almost frozen." ¶ 3 copies. ¶ July 2, 1900.

"The Cheyenne": "Indian on pony galloping with all four feet off the ground. Indian grasps spear in left hand and has war shield hung on his back." ¶ November 21, 1901. ¶ There is a variant of this.

"The Buffalo Signal": "Equestrian statue of Indian on pony with head held high and right front foot raised. Indian holds aloft a buffalo robe on a pole and has a gun across his lap." ¶ 1 copy only. ¶ December 17, 1901.

"Coming Through the Rye": "Bronze group of four cowboys on running horses. Men shooting pistols and shouting. Men represented as being on a carousal." ¶ October 8, 1902.

"The Mountain Man": "Man on horse coming down mountain side. Man fitted out with traps, knife, gun, cup, powder horn," etc. ¶ July 10, 1903.

"Sargeant": "Bust of Rough Rider Sargeant, height from bottom of base to rim of hat 10 inches. Stern face, sharp nose, heavy moustache, prominent chin, cheeks somewhat sunken, hat tilted on back of head. Handkerchief around neck." ¶ July 30, 1904.

"Polo": "Group of three horses and riders in game of polo. One horse has fallen and rider is caught under him. The second horse and rider are leaping directly over the fallen man. Third horse is standing with two hind legs upon the belly of fallen horse." ¶ July 21, 1904.

"The Rattlesnake": "Bronze group of cowboys on bronco—twenty inches high to top of head of rider. Rattlesnake on ground ready to attack horse. Horse shying and in a position denoting fright. Forefeet both in air," etc. ¶ January 18, 1905. ¶ There is a variant of this.

"Bronco Buster": Similar to the 1895 version except larger in scale. ¶ 1905.

"Dragoons—1850": "Two Dragoons and two Indians on horses in running fight. One single horse without rider in lead. Foremost soldier with raised sword in right hand ready to strike foremost Indian who is protecting himself with spear and shield." Etc. ¶ December 6, 1905.

"Paleolithic Man": "Being a representation of a human figure bordering on an ape, squatting and holding a clam in right hand and a club in left hand." ¶ June 30, 1906.

"The Outlaw": "Cowboy on a pitching bronco horse, same jumping in air and balanced on 'off' forefoot only. Cowboy leaning back with hand down on side of horse." ¶ May 3, 1906.

"The Horse Thief": "Nude Indian on horse holding buffalo skin with right arm as a protection. Buffalo robe flying in air. Horse running with three legs in air. Total height 30 inches, total length 27 inches." ¶ May 22, 1907.

"The Buffalo Horse": "Bronze group 36 inches high of a bull buffalo reared on hind legs with a pony on his nigh shoulder being tossed and above all the Indian rider being hurled upward with hands and one toe in contact with pony." Etc. ¶ December 12, 1907.

"The Fairmount Park Cowboy": "A bronze equestrian statue of cowboy on a Spanish horse. Reining sharply up, squatted behind—nigh front leg off ground. Cowboy thrown slightly forward away from saddle." ¶ April 27, 1908.
(Life size. Unveiled, Fairmount Park, Philadelphia, June 20, 1908)

"The Savage": "A bronze head of an Indian with long hair parted in middle, shells in ears and a wry expression on face. Total height 11 inches." ¶ December 14, 1908.

"Trooper of the Plains—1868": "A U. S. Cavalry Soldier, with drawn revolver, on a running horse, all feet off ground and supported by sage brush. 27 inches high, on base 20 inches long by 7½ inches wide." ¶ January 13, 1909.

"The Stampede": Bronze groups of stampeding cattle with mounted cowboy in their midst. ¶ April 13, 1910.

"Indian Dancer": Full figure of Indian dancer wearing ceremonial attire of elaborate bustle, belts of bells around ankles and below knees, wand in hand and decorative head-dress. ¶ Date not established.

Index

1. A CAVALRY OFFICER (from the series A BUNCH OF BUCKSKINS)

Pastel. Signed *Frederic Remington.* Undated. This series was reproduced in a portfolio of eight lithograph prints in color, 15″ x 20″, published by R. H. Russell, 1901.

Plate 1   A CAVALRY OFFICER

2.   A DASH FOR TIMBER

Oil. 48" x 84". Signed *Frederic Reming-ton.* Dated 1889. Exhibited 1889, National Academy Autumn Exhibition. Presented to Washington University, St. Louis, Mo., by the Fall Festivities Assoc. of that city, 1893. Although it was loaned to the St. Louis Museum the painting was owned by Washington University until May 1945 when it was sold by their order at auction in New York. Purchased by David Findlay, dealer, and sold to Amon G. Carter of Fort Worth, Texas, who has loaned the painting to the Fort Worth Club where it is now hung.

A fundamental tactic of frontier warfare was the use of trees, wherever available, from which to fight off Indian attacks.

Plate 2 A DASH FOR TIMBER

3. ANTELOPE HUNTING

    Oil. Signed *Frederic Remington*. Dated
1889. First reproduced in portfolio SPORT: OR
SHOOTING OR FISHING, published 1889 by Bradlee, Whidden Publishing Company, together
with companion plate, CANADA GOOSE SHOOTING,
by Remington, placing it as one of earliest Remington color prints.

Plate 3   ANTELOPE HUNTING

4.   CHARGE OF THE ROUGH RIDERS
     AT SAN JUAN HILL

   Oil. 36" x 60". Signed *Frederic Remington*.
Undated. Original in Remington Art Memorial,
Ogdensburg, New York. Used as black and white
illustration in Theodore Roosevelt's series of
articles, "The Rough Riders," for *Scribner's
Magazine,* April 1899. Color prints of the plate
were widely distributed and undoubtedly helped
to further Colonel Roosevelt's political career.

Plate 4   CHARGE OF THE ROUGH RIDERS AT SAN JUAN HILL

5.   A BREED (from the series A BUNCH OF
         BUCKSKINS)

      Pastel. Signed *Frederic Remington*. Dated
1901.

Plate 5   A BREED

6.   A TRAPPER (from the series A BUNCH
     OF BUCKSKINS)

   Pastel. Signed *Frederic Remington*. Undated.

Plate 6   A TRAPPER

7.   AN ARIZONA COWBOY (from the series A BUNCH OF BUCKSKINS)

Pastel. Signed *Frederic Remington*. Dated 1901. (The others in this series, not reproduced here, are: A SIOUX CHIEF, A CHEYENNE BUCK, AN ARMY PACKER, "OLD RAMON.")

Plate 7   AN ARIZONA COWBOY

8. THE SCOUT (from the series WESTERN
    TYPES)

    Oil. Signed *Frederic Remington*. Undated.
    One of a group of four paintings first repro-
    duced in color, in *Scribner's Magazine,* October
    1902. Soon afterward they were issued by Scrib-
    ner's as lithograph prints in color, 12″ x 16″.

Plate 8   THE SCOUT

9.   THE COWBOY (from the series
       WESTERN TYPES)

Oil. Signed *Frederic Remington*. Undated.

The full story of the sale of the original to
Remington's friend, John Howard, is told elsewhere in this volume. After asking and getting
what was then an exorbitant price for the painting, Remington destroyed the check by lighting
Mr. Howard's after-dinner cigar with it.

(The two WESTERN TYPES not reproduced
here are: THE COSSACK POST and THE HALF-
BREED.)

Plate 9   THE COWBOY

10.   CAUGHT IN THE CIRCLE
      Oil. Signed *Frederic Remington*. Undated.

First reproduced in *Collier's Weekly*, in color, December 7, 1901. Later appeared as the color plate in DONE IN THE OPEN, a book of Remington pictures accompanying verses by Owen Wister. Also published as a color print by Collier's.

The theme of frontiersmen making a desperate stand against Indians appealed strongly to Remington. This picture was not the first in which he used a similar motif, but proved to be one of the most popular.

Plate 10   CAUGHT IN THE CIRCLE

11.   HIS FIRST LESSON

Oil. Signed *Frederic Remington*. Undated.
First reproduced in *Collier's Weekly* in color, September 26, 1903.

This was the first canvas painted for Collier's under an agreement which gave the artist freedom from the restraint of illustrating. It was published by Collier's as a color print.

Plate 11   HIS FIRST LESSON

12. FIGHT FOR THE WATER HOLE

Oil. 27″ x 40″. Signed *Frederic Remington*. Undated. Now in the Museum of Fine Arts of Houston, Texas.

First reproduced in Collier's Weekly, in color, December 5, 1903. Color prints published by Collier's.

Routes across the desert were established by the position of the rare waterholes. Indian attacks often came as the caravans halted to rest and replenish their water supply.

Plate 12   FIGHT FOR THE WATER HOLE

13. THE PIONEERS

Oil. Signed *Frederic Remington*. Undated. First reproduced in *Collier's Weekly*, in color, February 13, 1904. Color prints published by Collier's.

Represents the pioneers' first advance up the rivers into the Indian country and belongs to an early era of Remington's graphic chronology of the Old West.

Plate 13   THE PIONEERS

14. AN OLD-TIME PLAINS FIGHT

Oil. 27" x 40". Signed *Frederic Remington*. Undated.

Original in Remington Art Memorial, Ogdensburg, New York. First reproduced, in black and white, in *Century Magazine*, April 1904. Later published as a color print.

Plate 14   AN OLD-TIME PLAINS FIGHT

15. THE EMIGRANTS

Oil. 30" x 45". Signed *Frederic Remington*. Undated.

Original in the Museum of Fine Arts of Houston, Texas. First reproduced in *Collier's Weekly*, in color, May 14, 1904. Color prints published by Collier's.

The subject is said to be based on the experience described to Remington by the boy shown standing in the foreground about to strike with his long pole at the war-bonneted Indian rider. The boy was left for dead, after being scalped, presumably the only survivor.

Plate 15   THE EMIGRANTS

16. NIGHT ATTACK ON A GOVERN-
MENT WAGON TRAIN

Oil. Signed *Frederic Remington*. Undated.
First reproduced in *Collier's Weekly*, in
color, June 11, 1904. Color prints published by
Collier's.

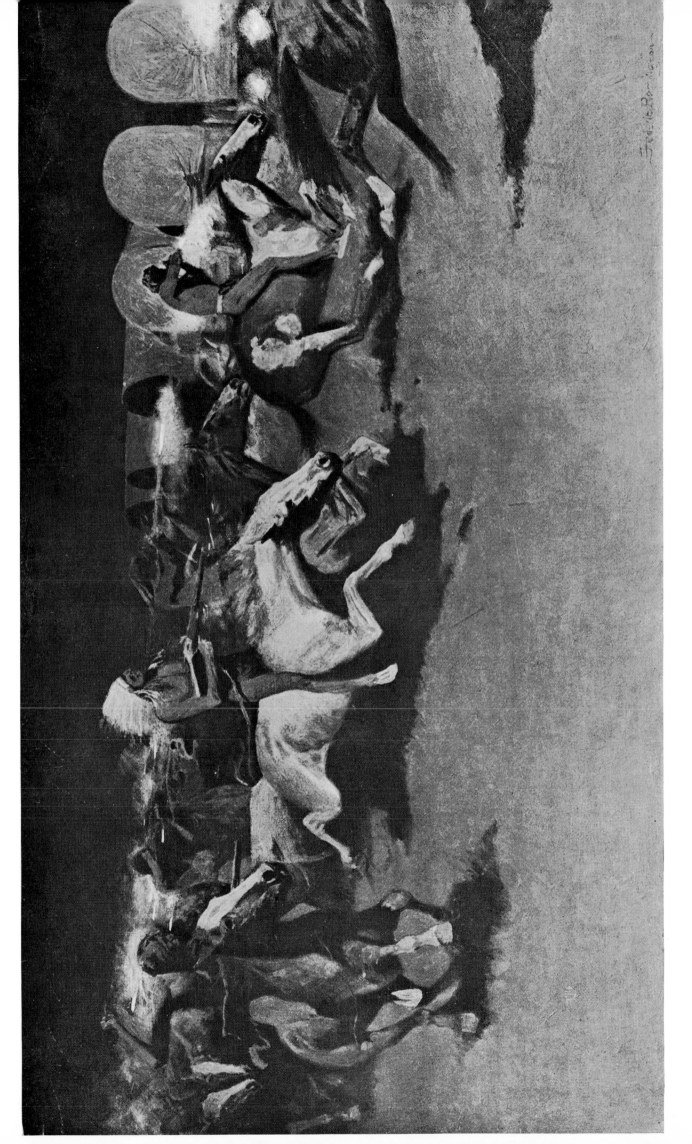

Plate 16   NIGHT ATTACK ON A GOVERNMENT WAGON TRAIN

17. AN ARGUMENT WITH
THE TOWN MARSHAL

Oil. Signed *Frederic Remington*. Undated.
Original owned by a private collector.

First reproduced in *Collier's Weekly*, in
color, February 11, 1905. Color prints published
by Collier's.

Plate 17   AN ARGUMENT WITH THE TOWN MARSHAL

18. EVENING ON A CANADIAN
     LAKE

Oil. Signed *Frederic Remington*. Undated. First reproduced in *Collier's Weekly*, in color, March 18, 1905. Color prints published by Collier's. One of the most popular of all Remington prints.

The canoe shown is the one which Remington himself used on the St. Lawrence River, and it is now stored in a barn in a town near the island, "Ingleneuk," where Remington spent a number of summers. The figures in the painting were posed for by two of the artist's friends.

Plate 18   EVENING ON A CANADIAN LAKE

19.   THE BUFFALO RUNNERS

Oil. Signed *Frederic Remington*. Undated. First reproduced in *Collier's Weekly*, in color, June 17, 1905. Color prints published by Collier's.

Authorities say there were once as many as 125,000,000 buffalo roaming our Western plains. The slaughter commenced with the coming of the white man; in the years 1872, 1873, 1874 an average of almost 5,000 were killed every day. By 1889 only 541 were left in the entire United States.

Plate 19 THE BUFFALO RUNNERS

20. THE CREEK INDIAN

Pastel. Signed *Frederic Remington*. Undated. First reproduced as the cover of *Collier's Weekly*, in color, December 12, 1903. Color prints published by Collier's.

The Creek Indians originally lived in what is now Alabama and Georgia, and were famous for their stalwart figures, grace of bearing and bravery in battle. Between 1836 and 1840 the Government moved a large part of the tribe westward into Indian Territory, now Oklahoma.

Plate 20   THE CREEK INDIAN

21. RADISSON AND GROSEILLIERS

(No. 4 of the GREAT EXPLORERS series)

Oil. Signed *Frederic Remington*. Undated. Original burned by the artist in 1908.

First reproduced in *Collier's Weekly*, in color, January 13, 1906. Color prints published by Collier's.

According to a notation in the artist's diary, he burned the entire Explorers series except LA VERENDRYE; and a similar fate overtook many of his other paintings.

These two Frenchmen were the first white men to visit the region that is now Minnesota. Radisson, the leader of the party, is shown standing in the birchbark canoe, with Groseilliers sitting beside him.

Plate 21   RADISSON & GROSEILLIERS

22.   MACKENZIE (No. 7 of the GREAT
      EXPLORERS series)

Oil. Signed *Frederic Remington*. Undated.
Original burned by the artist in 1908.

First reproduced in *Collier's Weekly,* in
color, April 14, 1906. Color prints published by
Collier's.

By the discovery of the great northern
river which bears his name and by sailing down
it to the Arctic Sea in 1789, Alexander Mackenzie proved there was no Northwest Passage
across North America. Four years later he crossed
the continent to the Western Sea (the Pacific
Ocean), a feat which his predecessors for three
hundred years had failed to accomplish and for
which he was knighted by the King of England.

(Others in the GREAT EXPLORERS series,
not reproduced here: CABECA DE VACA, HER-
NANDO DE SOTO, CORONADO, LA SALLE, LA
VERENDRYE, LEWIS AND CLARK, ZEBULON PIKE,
JEDEDIAH SMITH.)

Plate 22   MACKENZIE

23. THE HOWL OF THE WEATHER

Oil. 26″ x 36″. Signed *Frederic Remington*. Undated. Original in Remington Art Memorial, Ogdensburg, New York.

First reproduced in *Collier's Weekly*, in color, February 16, 1907. Color prints published by Collier's.

Plate 23   THE HOWL OF THE WEATHER

24. DOWNING THE NIGH LEADER

Oil. Signed *Frederic Remington.* Undated. Original owned by a private collector in New York, N. Y.

First reproduced in *Collier's Weekly*, in color, April 20, 1907. Color prints published by Collier's.

Such violent scenes as these were the source and inspiration of our Western movies.

Plate 24   DOWNING THE NIGH LEADER

25.   BRINGING HOME THE
      NEW COOK

Oil. Signed *Frederic Remington*. Undated.
First reproduced in *Collier's Weekly*, in
color, November 2, 1907. Color prints published
by Collier's.

The advent of a new cook was an occasion
for jubilation on the big cattle ranches, especially if the former cook had been unpopular or
incompetent.

Plate 25   BRINGING HOME THE NEW COOK

26. CEREMONY OF THE SCALPS

Oil. Signed *Frederic Remington*. Undated.
First reproduced in *Collier's Weekly*, in
color, June 13, 1908. Color prints published by
Collier's.

In this grim celebration the scalps are
attached to a ceremonial pole which is held over-
head by the chieftain, who rides at the head of
his warriors.

Plate 26 CEREMONY OF THE SCALPS

27. APACHES LISTENING

Oil. 19″ x 26″. Signed *Frederic Remington*. Undated, but it is known to have been painted during the last few months of Remington's life, in 1909. Original in Remington Art Memorial, Ogdensburg, New York.

This painting has never before been reproduced in any periodical or book. The Apaches and their arid land had a strong appeal for Remington, who made numerous trips into their country.

Plate 27   APACHES LISTENING

28. THE SUN DANCE

Oil. 27" x 40". Signed *Frederic Remington*. Undated, but it is known to have been painted in 1909, the last year of Remington's life. Original in the Remington Art Memorial, Ogdensburg, New York.

This painting has never before been reproduced in any periodical or book. It presents braves suspended in air by reatas, the free ends of which are fastened to skewers inserted in the skin of their breasts or backs; a common practice during the solemn Sun Dance ceremony of the Plains Indians.

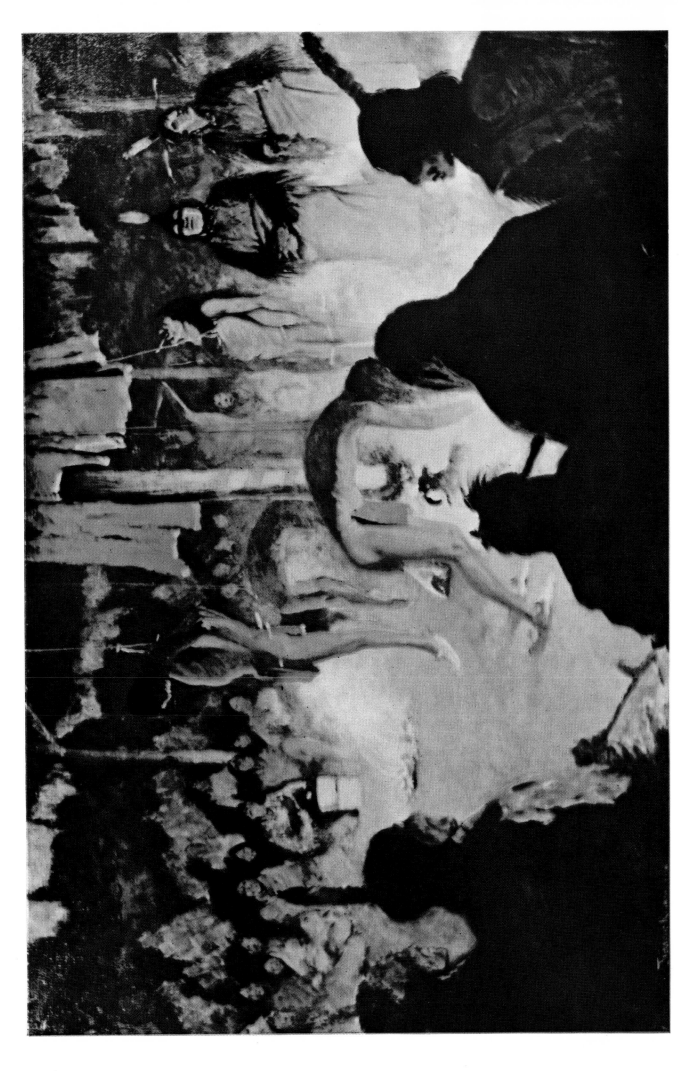

Plate 28   THE SUN DANCE

29. HAULING IN THE GILL NET

Oil. 19" x 26". Signed *Frederic Remington*. Undated, but it is known to have been painted shortly before Remington's death in 1909. Original in Remington Art Memorial, Ogdensburg, New York.

This painting has never before been reproduced in any periodical or book.

Plate 29   HAULING IN THE GILL NET

30. THE SENTINEL

Oil. 26″ x 36″. Signed *Frederic Remington*. Undated, but known to be one of the last paintings done by Remington. Original in Remington Art Memorial, Ogdensburg, New York.

This painting has never before been reproduced in any book, although it was published as a color print.

Plate 30   THE SENTINEL

31.   THE BUFFALO HUNTER

Oil. Signed *Frederic Remington*. Undated.
First reproduced in *Collier's Weekly*, in
color, July 1, 1911, under title THE BUFFALO
RUNNER. Color print, titled THE BUFFALO
HUNTER, published by Collier's.

The central figures are the same as those
in Remington's bronze, THE BUFFALO HORSE.

Plate 31   THE BUFFALO HUNTER

32.   CUTTING OUT PONY HERDS

Oil. Signed *Frederic Remington.* Dated 1908. First reproduced in *Collier's Weekly*, in color, February 1, 1913. Color prints published by Collier's.

Plate 32   CUTTING OUT PONY HERDS

Plate 33. A RUNNING BUCKER. From *Drawings,* 1897

Plate 34.   "Such as these the shapes they painted . . ."   "Thus the birch canoe was builded . . ."

Illustrations from Longfellow's *The Song of Hiawatha,* Houghton, Mifflin & Co., 1891

Plate 35.   THE PONY WAR DANCE. From *Drawings*, 1897

Plate 36. THE BORDERLAND OF THE OTHER TRIBE. *From Drawings, 1897*

Plate 37. HER CALF. From *Drawings*, 1897

Plate 28   PROTECTING THE WAGON TRAIN   *From Frederic Remington*   1907

Plate 39. A MISDEAL. From *Drawings*, 1897

Plate 40. TWILIGHT OF THE INDIAN. From *Drawings*, 1897

Plate 41.   THE BRONCO BUSTER. 1895

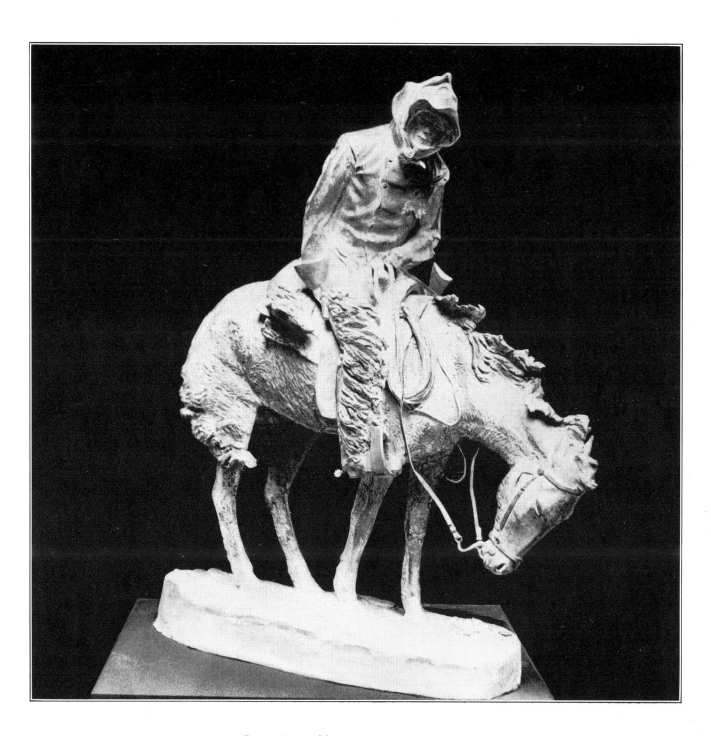

Plate 42.   THE NORTHER. 1900

The clay model from which the castings were made. Photograph by Frederic Remington

Plate 43.   COMING THROUGH THE RYE. 1902

Plate 44.   THE MOUNTAIN MAN. 1903

Plate 45.
Above: DRAGOONS — 1850. Modeled in 1905.

Below: THE INDIAN DANCER. Date unknown

Plate 46.   THE OUTLAW. 1906

Plate 47. THE RATTLESNAKE. 1905

Plate 48. THE BUFFALO HORSE. 1907